ANCIENT ENGLISH HOUSES

CHRISTOPHER SIMON SYKES

Ancient English Houses

1240–1612

CHATTO & WINDUS

LONDON

Published in 1988 by
Chatto & Windus Limited
30 Bedford Square
London WC1B 3RP

A CIP catalogue record for this book is available
from the British Library

ISBN 0 7011 3176 4

Photoset in Linotron Palatino by
Rowland Phototypesetting Limited
Bury St Edmunds, Suffolk

Colour origination by Waterden Reproductions Limited

Printed in Great Britain by
Roundwood Press Limited, Warwick

ACKNOWLEDGEMENTS

In the course of writing this book, I visited
not only the houses included but many more which, for one reason or another,
I have not been able to squeeze in.
To all those kind owners who welcomed and, in many cases, fed and watered me,
I extend my heartfelt gratitude.
My thanks are also due to
Mr and Mrs Michael Heathcote-Amory,
Lord and Lady Eliot,
Mr and Mrs Simon Elliot,
Lord and Lady Tollemache,
Lord and Lady Ivor Windsor,
Lord Neidpath and Mr David Hart,
all of whom provided beds for the night during my researches.
I would also like to thank the staff and administrators of
the various National Trust houses included in the book
and, finally, to give a special mention to all the staff at the London Library
where most of the manuscript was written.

Contents

HOUSES OPEN TO THE PUBLIC

The following houses in the book
are open to the public.
Some, marked NT, belong to the National Trust.
Those not mentioned on the list are strictly private.

Stokesay Castle, Craven Arms, Shropshire. (05882) 2544
Markenfield Hall, Ripon, Yorks
Ightham Mote, Sevenoaks, Kent. (0732) 810378 (NT)
Lower Brockhampton Manor, Bringsty, Herefordshire. (0905) 23296 (NT)
Broughton Castle, Banbury, Oxon. (0295) 62624
Little Sodbury Manor, Chipping Sodbury, Gloucs. (0454) 312232
Great Chalfield Manor, Melksham, Wilts. (0225) 782239 (NT)
Oxburgh Hall, King's Lynn, Norfolk. (036621) 258 (NT)
Cotehele, St Dominick, Saltash, Cornwall. (0579) 50434 (NT)
Otley Hall, Ipswich, Suffolk. (0449) 613535
Athelhampton Hall, Athelhampton, Dorset. (030584) 363
Compton Castle, Marldon, Devon. (08047) 2112 (NT)
Westwood Manor, Bradford-on-Avon, Wilts. (02216) 3374 (NT)
Poundisford Park, Taunton, Somerset. (082342) 244
Cadhay, Ottery St Mary, Devon. (040481) 2432
Pitchford Hall, Shrewsbury, Shropshire. Open for B & B. (06944) 205
Wolfeton House, Dorchester, Dorset. (0305) 63500
Rainthorpe Hall, Flordon, Norfolk. (05084) 70618
Benthall Hall, Broseley, Shropshire. (0952) 882159 (NT)
Stanway House, Broadway, Gloucs. (038673) 469
Hardwick Hall, Chesterfield, Derbyshire. (0246) 850430 (NT)
Chastleton House, Moreton-in-Marsh, Gloucs. (060874) 355
Burton Agnes, Bridlington, Yorks. (026289) 324

Introduction

England is a country which is still full of mysterious and secret places. Not long ago, while travelling through Essex, a wrong turning led me into a maze of narrow lanes to the south of the village of Felstead. While attempting to extricate myself from this tortuous network, my curiosity was aroused by a glimpse of what appeared to be the top of some kind of tower peeping out of a distant belt of trees. The delightful prospect of discovering some unknown folly persuaded me to investigate further and, after taking several wrong turnings and passing some rather derelict-looking farm buildings, I eventually found myself standing before a pair of large and firmly padlocked iron gates. Beyond them, an unkempt drive with grass sprouting through its surface led up to an impressive, two-storey red-brick gatehouse, flanked by polygonal, embattled turrets, to the left of which stood an adjoining wing, also crenellated, around whose transomed windows there climbed a beautiful old-fashioned rose. After peering through the rusty bars for some time and noticing a vista of twisty chimneys and more turrets to the north, I was

encouraged to attempt to gain entry, and boldly blew my horn. After some time, the owner appeared and agreed to allow me to wander around and take a few photographs. It was an exciting moment, for behind the gatehouse, in the middle of what must once have been an inner quadrangle, stood an even finer, three-storey, tower, with octagonal turrets at each corner. I then discovered that the buildings upon which I had so unexpectedly stumbled were all that remains of a great Tudor palace built by the notorious Richard Rich, Solicitor-General to Henry VIII.

Since, in recent years, the pre-Inigo Jones period has rather fallen out of fashion, such romantic gems of early English architecture tend to be overlooked. Yet the country abounds with them. Some, such as Ightham Mote in Kent, or Cranborne Manor in Dorset, are quite well known, but the majority, which remain relatively undiscovered, encapsulate that period of architecture to which Virginia Woolf referred when she wrote, 'Chatsworth is in England, but Knole is of England.'

The north tower from the churchyard

Stokesay Castle

'A friend of mine, an American who knew this country,' wrote Henry James in 1905, 'had told me not to fail, while I was in the neighbourhood, to go to Stokesay and two or three other places. "Edward IV and Elizabeth," he said, "are still hanging about there." So admonished, I made a point of going at least to Stokesay, and I saw quite what my friend meant . . . I have rarely had, for a couple of hours, the sensation of dropping back personally into the past so straight as while I lay on the grass beside the well in the little sunny court of this small castle and lazily appreciated the still definite details of medieval life. The place is a capital example of a small gentilhommiere of the thirteenth century.'

Henry James's impressions of this extraordinary and romantic place must echo those of countless others making their first visit to Stokesay. It is one of the earliest and best examples in the country of a medieval fortified manor house.

The hall

The origins of Stokesay go back to the days of William the Conqueror when the manor, then called simply Stoke (meaning a dairy farm), was granted to a family called Lacy as part of great possessions which fell to their share after the conquest. They held the land till some time before 1115, when it was granted to a certain Theodoric de Say, whose family originated from Sai in Normandy and who gave their name to Stokesay. It was one of the Say family who built, about 1240, the earliest part of the house, which is the lower two storeys of the north tower. The moat, too, dates from this period. The main work, however, was carried out some forty years later by the next owner of Stokesay, Lawrence de Ludlow, who was the richest wool merchant of the day and who had decided to invest some of his profits in land. He bought the property around 1281 and at once set about transforming it from a mere moated keep into a residence fit for a prosperous merchant.

The first work to be carried out was the construction of the hall, which is the building immediately facing one after passing through the gatehouse. It is a tall and striking structure, with a high-pitched roof of stone slates broken by four gables, beneath three of which are high ecclesiastical windows with arched heads and transomed lights. The entrance is through a great arched doorway in the northernmost of the gables, and this leads into a huge room, some fifty-two feet long, thirty-one feet wide and thirty-four feet high. It is full of light, owing to the unusual size of the windows which descend almost to the ground, where they are fitted with seats in the thickness of the walls. The steeply-pitched roof, with its double collar-beams and curved collar-braces, rests upon masonry pillars which rise from stone corbels set between the windows. There is no fireplace. Blackened beams bear witness to the log fires which would have blazed from a central brazier standing on the octagonal centrally-placed open stone hearth, sending their smoke aloft to the roof. From the north-west corner a rough wooden staircase of

The castle and church from the south-west. The north tower (left) was begun in 1240; then comes the hall range (centre), begun 1285; and the south tower (right), begun 1291

A charming wooden window in the solar

solid oak rises diagonally, its flights and landings being arranged to serve the odd levels of the rooms of the old north tower, most of which would have served as offices.

De Ludlow next added a solar wing, in the form of a cross-wing with separate floor adjoining the hall to the south. This consisted of an undercroft with a room above it 'open to the rays of the sun', to which the lord and his immediate circle could withdraw from the hall after meals for privacy, though they were still able to keep an eye on what was going on below through the two peepholes in the north wall. Access to the solar was by an outside timber staircase sheltered by a gabled penthouse roof. The building of such a facility is indicative of how, even in wild Welsh Border country, the concept was developing of houses being comfortable homes as well as secure places in which to hide away.

In 1291, however, de Ludlow, never underestimating the dangerous times in which he lived, followed up these additions with a request to Edward I for a licence to fortify his new house. This was granted, and the result was the massive embattled south tower and a curtain wall built to a height of thirty-four feet above the moat. Although the latter has virtually disappeared, a small section of it can still be seen at the south-east corner of the tower. As for the south tower itself, it is an irregular polygon of three storeys, sixty-six feet high and thirty-nine feet across, and originally its entrance was on the first floor by way of a drawbridge from a platform outside the solar. It had no direct access to any of the other buildings and was purely for defence against the bands of marauders who inhabited the strip of country which divided England from Wales. It inspired Henry James to further reveries: '. . . it was not difficult to pursue the historic vision through the dark, roughly circular rooms of the tower itself, and up the corkscrew staircase of the same to that most charming part of every old castle, where visions must leap away off the battlements to elude you – the bright, dizzy platform at the tower top, the place where the castle standard hung

The solar, begun about 1285, to which the lord and his immediate circle could withdraw for privacy

A peephole in the solar through which the lord could keep an eye on the goings on in the hall below

and the vigilant inmates surveyed the approaches. Here always, you really overtake the impression of the place – here, in the sunny stillness, it seems to pause, panting a little, and give itself up.'

The whole building operation was completed by about 1305 when the approach to Stokesay was almost certainly across a drawbridge, though there appears to have been some kind of stone tower, of an earlier date, on the site of the present gatehouse. The latter, which is half-timbered and noted for the delightful decoration and carving of its timbers, is much later than the main buildings, dating from the late sixteenth century. Stokesay was inhabited until the early nineteenth century. Its future was assured when, in 1869, it was sold to a rich glove manufacturer, Mr J. D. Allcroft, who set about the task of restoring and preserving it, a job which has been continued by his descendants.

View across the moat of the sixteenth-century gatehouse and earlier outbuildings at Markenfield

Markenfield Hall

Though Markenfield Hall is situated only a short distance outside the city of Ripon, its existence is still relatively unknown even in the neighbourhood. An insignificant signpost directs the determined traveller off the main Harrogate to Ripon road and on to a farm track which winds its way between cornfields and beast-filled meadows. After a mile or so, one catches a glimpse of stone buildings to the right, half hidden by the rise in the ground, the first clue that the wrong road has not been taken. The track then climbs a gentle slope and soon terminates in the middle of a busy farmyard. Here one has one's first view, in the form of a bridge across a moat and a lovely gatehouse, of part of an extraordinary medieval survival, a fourteenth-century country house that has altered remarkably little since it was first built.

Markenfield would not always have been so hard to find. Up to the middle of the eighteenth century it dominated the old road south from Ripon, which then ran beneath its battlements, and, situated as it is upon a slight hill, nobody could then have doubted its importance. It

The medieval great hall, one of the earliest of its kind in the country

14

One of the hall windows

was built by John de Markenfield, a cleric and leading official of Edward II, out of money from church benefices which he had accumulated as he grew in favour with the King. This reached its high point in 1310 when he was appointed Chancellor of the Exchequer. The same year he was granted licence to crenellate, a visible sign of how far he had progressed and necessary for the protection of his new house against the sudden raids which were commonplace at that time. These might have been carried out by a local rival jealous of his success, or by somebody with a grudge, for by all accounts de Markenfield was, even by the standards of the day, a pretty unsavoury character. He was involved at one time or another with cases of intimidation and rape, and his close friendship with the King's favourite, Piers Gaveston, had made him many enemies.

The house built by de Markenfield consists of a tall L-shaped castellated block, the west wing of which is pierced by a pair of two-light transomed windows each with a quatrefoil at the top. These light the great hall which occupies the whole of the first floor and is one of the earliest of its kind in the country. It stands above an undercroft, and was originally reached by means of an external stone staircase, the position of which can still be seen from the chevron which remains to the left of the hall windows. The present internal staircase was a nineteenth-century addition. The roof too is modern, though the corbels remain upon which the original open timber roof would have rested. East of the great hall is the solar, with an adjoining garderobe, while to the south lies the chapel, with another chamber, possibly de Markenfield's own, beyond, and a newel stair leading up to the roof in between. Initially the rooms in the undercroft would all have been vaulted, as can be seen from the small section which has survived in the north-east corner. These would have been various offices, though it is likely that the kitchen was at first in a separate building. The lower ranges, which surround the forecourt to the east and west, were

The sixteenth-century gatehouse. The site on which it stands may not be the original one, which is more likely to have been in the middle of the farmhouse wing, where the remains of a large arch can be seen

Overleaf: John de Markenfield's main building, one of the finest surviving fourteenth-century houses in England

all farm buildings. Of these, the east wing, which contains the present farmhouse, is thought to be the earlier of the two and was probably castellated.

The de Markenfields inhabited this house till the latter half of the sixteenth century, during which time it was considerably remodelled inside to provide more rooms and greater comfort; a new kitchen to the west of the main block was one of the more important additions. Though most of this work was carried out during the fifteenth century, the present gatehouse dates from a century later, not long before the family were disgraced and their land confiscated. In 1569 Thomas de Markenfield, along with his neighbour Richard Conyers of Norton Conyers, rode at the head of an army which first gathered in the forecourt at Markenfield, then marched to hear mass at Ripon Cathedral, and finally joined the Earl of Northumberland's forces to march south with the intention of freeing Mary Queen of Scots and restoring the faith of Rome. It was a disastrous expedition, and the Rising of the North, as it became known, was swiftly quashed. Somewhat miraculously, considering the fate which befell most of his

fellow conspirators, along with eight hundred of their tenants, de Markenfield escaped the gallows and fled abroad. His house and lands were subsequently granted by Queen Elizabeth to Thomas Egerton, Master of the Rolls.

Evidently Egerton never made Markenfield his principal residence, for it was not long before it was being used solely as a farmhouse. By the middle of the eighteenth century it was in very poor condition, at which point it was bought by Fletcher Norton, a rich and successful local lawyer whose prosperity is best explained by the nickname, Sir Bullface Double Fees, awarded to him during his time as Attorney-General. Though he, too, never lived in the house, preferring Grantley Hall, his own home in the neighbourhood, he did at least give it a new roof and made sure the building was structurally sound. However his descendant, Lord Grantley, the present owner, after several years spent restoring the main block, has moved in. He is thus the first owner to have inhabited the house for four hundred years.

A pair of
two-light
transomed
windows
pierce the
west wing
of Marken-
field

The outer quadrangle, through which the house was originally approached. The sixteenth-century half-timbered buildings are now in use as cottages

The great hall. The five-light window in the west wall was added in the early sixteenth century. Before that the only light would have come from gaps in the ceiling for the smoke from the central hearth to pass through, and a two-light window in the east wall

Ightham Mote

The very approach to Ightham Mote is romantic, down narrow, leafy Kentish lanes where the view is all but hidden by tall hedges. Suddenly one rounds a corner, and there below lies a vision of the ideal English manor house. Standing foursquare round a courtyard, with a crenellated gatehouse, and built of oak timber and Kentish ragstone, it rises sheer out of a square moat. There is an air of secrecy about Ightham Mote, tucked away as it is in a secluded hollow and surrounded by woods, which gives some credence to the legend that it escaped ransacking during the Civil War because the party of Cromwell's soldiers who came to carry out the task got lost and turned their attentions to another house instead.

The broad moat is a reminder of the age in which the house was built, a time of growing social and economic unrest which was to culminate in the Peasants' Revolt of 1381. It was in 1340 that the earliest recorded owner, Sir Thomas Cawne, lived there, and the oldest parts of the house are almost certainly attributable to him. Lying on the eastern side of the quadrangle, they make up the typical dwelling of a fourteenth-century knight. Having crossed the moat by a stone bridge, where formerly a drawbridge must have stood, and passed through the gatehouse, one finds oneself in a cobbled courtyard. Directly opposite is the stone hall which would have formed the nucleus of the original house. It is remarkable for the height of its open timber roof of trussed rafters, thirty-seven and a half feet, with a single stone arch spanning it towards the south end, repeated in timber on the end walls. All the supporting arches spring from charming carved corbels representing figures of varying grotesqueness who carry the weight of the roof upon their shoulders. An arched doorway at the north end of the eastern wall leads both to the crypt and up a seventeenth-century staircase to the original chapel and the solar, both of which have open timber roofs.

In 1480 the then owner, Sir Richard Haut, decided that the building needed both enlarging and improving, and he increased the gatehouse by two stories, added rooms on either side, and built the south and west wings. Twenty

The Tudor chapel. The ribs of the barrel-vaulted ceiling are painted with chevrons in the Tudor livery colours of green and white or silver. The panels in between are richly ornamented with family arms and those of the King and Queen

A corbel in the shape of a grotesque female figure upon whose shoulders rests the weight of the roof

years later his son Edward put a large five-light window in the hall, and substituted a fireplace and chimney for the open hearth, a reflection of new ideas about comfort. The final flurry of building at Ightham Mote was carried out by Richard Clement who bought it for £400 in 1521, and set about an elaborate scheme of modernisation. He made the chapel into a domestic extension by inserting a new floor and chimneys, turning the existing tall window into two, and creating an upper and lower bedroom. He squared off the courtyard by filling in the north side of the quadrangle with a new chapel, built of timberwork above an open cloister and largely overhanging the moat. It is one of the glories of the house, its outstanding feature being the wooden barrel-vaulted roof.

That Ightham Mote has not joined the ranks of the lost mansions of England is something of a miracle, for the house fell into disrepair in the nineteen forties, and by the early fifties its future was seriously in question. Its survival owes much to one man's boyhood dream. Charles Henry Robinson, an American businessman, had visited the Mote as a child and had fallen in love with it. On a trip to England in 1953 he was reminded of his former passion when he saw a print of the house in a London art-dealer's. Hearing that the house was for sale, he lost no time in going to look at it, and promptly bought it. A careful plan of restoration then began, and the following year he bequeathed the property to the National Trust, thus guaranteeing its future.

The newel post of the Jacobean staircase carved in the shape of a Saracen's head, the crest of the Selby family who owned the house for 300 years

25

The east front

A view from the south-west. The moat runs all round the house, and is crossed by three bridges, one of which was probably a drawbridge leading to the main entrance

The gatehouse. The thin slit to the left of the arch was a device for holding parley with suspected enemies

Brinsop from the south-west. To the left is the former chapel, built in the early fifteenth century. To its right is a timber-framed building, dating from the sixteenth century, while the block on the far right was built during the reign of Queen Anne

Brinsop Court

In March 1879 the Reverend Francis Kilvert made a journey to Brinsop Court, near Hereford. 'A fine sweet gleam,' he later wrote, 'lit up the grand old manor house and the lawn and the two snow white swans on the flowing water of the moat. On the lawn grew the cedar planted by William Wordsworth the poet. Young Mr Edwards [the tenant of the farm] was carpentering in the greenhouse. He courteously took us into a noble sitting-room, Turkey carpetted and nicely furnished with a fine painting of the poet over the chimney-piece . . . [He] showed us the grand old banquetting hall reached by a flight of exterior steps from the courtyard. It is now a granary. Opposite were the Chapel and Armoury. Mr Edwards said he had heard his father say that when he first came down to Brinsop out of Radnorshire he rode across the moat over the old drawbridge.'

The old drawbridge, long since demolished and replaced by two bridges, was a relic of the early days of Brinsop Court, whose history goes back to the fourteenth century. Built of red sandstone and situated in wooded

The south front with the hall in the foreground

hilly country to the north-west of Hereford, it is one of the best examples of a large moated manor house of its date in the country. Its builders were the Tirrell family, who had held the manor since the days of King John, the first stone probably having been laid by Ralph Tirrell c.1300–10. Of this early structure only a fragment remains, in the north range of the present house, where three two-light windows of the period can be seen, just to the east of the entrance. The next flurry of building activity took place c.1320–30 when the north and a low west range were completed. Finally a hall range to the south was begun c.1340, the eastern half containing the great hall being constructed first, with a solar to the west following shortly afterwards.

The next family to leave their mark on Brinsop were the Danseys, who became lords of the manor early in the fifteenth century, and were to remain so for a further 400 years. Soon after their occupation they surmounted the main entrance with a stone tower and built a chapel in the north wing. In the sixteenth century they replaced the low west wing with a much higher timber-framed building, carrying out further rebuilding in the southern half of this range towards the end of the next century, while the eighteenth-century Danseys refronted in brick that part

of the west wing overlooking the courtyard. The last additions to the house were made in 1913 when the new owner, H. D. Astley, built an east range, thus enclosing the courtyard. He also carried out a sensitive programme of restoration to the hall, which can be seen today much as it was when first built. This room is without doubt one of the finest surviving examples of a fourteenth-century first-floor hall in England. The open timber roof is particularly impressive.

Brinsop remains an exceptionally picturesque house and, though its great entrance tower has disappeared, pulled down in the nineteenth century to 'assist in building a wall round the stables', the north front retains much of its original appearance. The moat too, which is unusual for the way in which it varies in width at different places, has changed little. It is a romantic place, and one can quite understand how it caught the imagination of William Wordsworth, who made several visits between 1827 and 1845, when it was in the tenancy of his brother-in-law. It was here that he wrote his poems on Bishopstone and Ledbury. He also planted the cedar mentioned by Kilvert, at the south-west corner of the house. Until it was blown down, on Boxing Day 1916, it was known as Wordsworth's Cedar.

One of the two-light windows in the hall. The stone seats in the embrasures are a charming feature

The first-floor great hall, its massive wooden beams spanning the width of the room like immense girders

Lower Brockhampton Manor

Everyone who thinks of England as a country full of quaint thatched cottages and 'ye olde oake' timber-framed mansions must catch their breath when they first set eyes on Lower Brockhampton Manor. They will have had to search hard to find it in its remote setting two miles off the road from Leominster to Worcester, down in the woods beyond Brockhampton Park and at the foot of a small valley. But it will have been worthwhile, for this is the genuine article, the original picturesque and ancient timbered house. It is even surrounded by a moat.

Lower Brockhampton, which means 'the farm of the dwellers on the brook', is one of the finest examples of a black and white manor in the Welsh Marches. A two-storey house, it was probably built sometime between 1380 and 1400 by John Domulton, a descendant of the Brockhampton family who were the owners of the property during the previous two centuries. The design was an H-shaped plan with cross wings at the east and west ends, the latter having since been demolished. The exterior is striking for its elaborately carved bargeboards and its

timber-framing, some of which consists of narrowly set uprights, the rest of large square panels. Inside there is a good example of a medieval open hall with an interesting openwork timber roof and a timbered screens passage.

But without doubt the most delightful feature of Lower Brockhampton, and that for which the house is best remembered by almost all who visit it, is the pretty timber-framed gatehouse. It is, along with that at Stokesay Castle, one of the few timber gatehouses to have survived. It was erected late in the fifteenth century and has an upper storey projecting outwards from curved brackets which spring from angle posts with moulded capitals. The bargeboards decorating the gables are carved with a design of trailing vine leaves. The fact that it also leans slightly to one side, as if at any moment it might take off and totter across the lawn, is almost too good to be true.

A view of Lower Brockhampton from the south-east. The long, low house is late fourteenth century, but the gatehouse is late fifteenth century

The vaulted south corridor which leads from the private apartments to the hall

The gatehouse showing the sole surviving stretch of the medieval defensive wall, which had both crenellations and a wall walk

Broughton Castle

When Celia Fiennes visited Broughton Castle in the latter half of the seventeenth century, she described it as 'an old house moted round and a parke and gardens, but are much left to decay and ruine.' She had a special interest in Broughton, for it belonged to her half-brother William, third Viscount Saye and Sele. The Fiennes family, who have remained in residence to this day, first came to Broughton in 1451.

The origins of Broughton Castle go back to the middle of the thirteenth century when a John of Broughton held the manor. The vaulted undercroft of the former great chamber, now the dining room, and the adjoining undercroft of the chapel certainly date from this period, and suggest the existence then of an L-shaped first-floor hall house. In 1300 John's descendant, Sir John of Broughton, embarked on a grandiose scheme of remodelling, building a spectacular new hall, moated round and separated from the earlier house by a slight gap. In 1315 his son added a chapel, two storeys high with another two-storey block adjoining it, linked by a system of vaulted corridors and double staircases. The third stage of evolution took place in the early fifteenth century and was related to the licence to crenellate granted in 1406 to Sir Thomas Wykeham, son of the celebrated William of Wykeham, Bishop of Winchester and Chancellor of England, who had purchased the house in 1377. He enclosed the manor with a defensive curtain which had both crenellations and a wall walk, a stretch of which still survives by the entrance tower.

Much of the medieval house still remains, though incorporated within the considerable alterations carried out by Sir Richard Fiennes and his son in the latter half of the sixteenth century. The chapel excepted, they virtually rebuilt the principal rooms, replacing the open timber roof of the hall with a lowered flat ceiling above which two new storeys were constructed, and creating new staircases by the addition of two gabled projections on the south front. On the north front they added two symmetrical bay windows with a central oriel. The younger Fiennes completed the new work in about 1598 with the addition of a projecting west wing of two storeys to balance the medieval east

The semi-octagonal interior porch in the Oak Room. It carries a Latin inscription which reads QUOD OLIM FUIT MEMINISSE MINIME JUVAT, 'There is little joy in remembrance of the past'

wing. Since that date the house has changed structurally very little.

From the eastern end of the hall the medieval vaulted south corridor leads to the dining room which has a fine quadripartite vault and linenfold panelling, and beyond to the former sixteenth-century kitchen wing, now family apartments. At the screens end a Tudor arch leads to the west wing, with its projecting central bay, containing two beautiful light rooms. That on the ground floor is the lovely Oak Room. Above it lies the White Room, which has an elaborate ceiling dated 1599 with pendants and moulded strapwork.

In the early nineteenth century Broughton Castle almost fell victim to the extravagances of Baron William Thomas, the fifteenth Lord Saye and Sele, a notorious rake. His reign ended with a sale of the contents of the castle, right down to the swans on the moat. In 1888 bankruptcy in the family was only averted by the efforts of younger brothers and various cousins, an act reflecting the powerful feelings held by the family for their home down the centuries, and still held today by the twenty-first of the line of Saye and Sele.

The gatehouse

Decorative corbels in the south corridor

The great hall, which measures fifty-four feet by thirty feet, is medieval in plan. The windows are eighteenth century

Overleaf: the south elevation of Broughton from across the moat. The two projecting wings contain the staircases

The west elevation.
The central block with porch is
the earliest part of the house, built
in the 1420s. The north wing
(to the left) was added in the late
fifteenth century, while the
buildings to the south date
from the early sixteenth century

Little Sodbury Manor

On 25 July, 1535, King Henry VIII and Anne Boleyn left
Thornbury Castle in Gloucestershire, where they had
spent the preceding ten days, and set out for Bristol. But
Sir John Walsh, a local landowner who had been at court
since the King was a boy and who had acted as his Cham-
pion at his coronation in 1509, hearing of an outbreak of
plague in that city, intercepted the King and persuaded
him to come and stay at his own house instead. More than
half a century earlier Little Sodbury Manor had already
given shelter to a queen and two kings, when Margaret of
Anjou, the wife of Henry VI, passed the night of 29 April
1471 there, followed two days later by her Yorkist enemies,
Edward IV and his brother the Duke of Gloucester, the
future Richard III.

The site on which Little Sodbury stands is of great
antiquity, having been continuously inhabited since the
Bronze Age. It is mentioned as early as the first century by
the Roman historian Tacitus, and takes its name, which
derives from the Saxon words 'sod', meaning south, and
'bury', a camp, from the fortifications on the crest of the

Ceiling braces in the late
medieval great hall

hill above the house. These the Romans had converted from a Bronze Age camp to form part of a defensive line of forts to protect the area from marauding Welsh tribes. In 577 it is recorded that a Saxon army made their head-quarters at Little Sodbury before the Battle of Dyrham, and in the time of Edward the Confessor a dwelling house arose on the site, the property of a Saxon named Aluard. Though no trace of this remains, the present manor stands on the same spot.

It is a dramatic setting, the house clinging precariously to the slope of a steep hill, overlooking the town of Chipping Sodbury with distant views beyond to the Severn estuary and the Welsh hills. It dates back to the early fifteenth century, when a family called Stanshaw, who owned great estates in the area, became lords of the manor of Little Sodbury and built there a large unfortified manor house. This was grouped round a courtyard, now the West Lawn, and approached from the south through a gatehouse. All that remains of it are the entrance porch and the great hall. The latter is generally acknowledged to be one of the finest late medieval great halls in England. Its proportions are unusual owing to the height of the walls and the extreme steepness of the open timber roof with its arched braced collar-beams, elaborately moulded purlins and no fewer than four ascending tiers of wind-braces. The roof rests on stone corbels with carved angels holding shields (which are lucky to have survived, con-sidering the habit of the father of the present owner of taking pot shots with his 12-bore at jackdaws which had come in down the chimney). By the time Henry VIII made his visit, the house had been much enlarged and im-proved, both by Sir John and his father, John Walsh Esq., into whose hands it had come in 1492. These alterations included the building of a new kitchen and another wing to the south of the hall.

Sir John Walsh was responsible for introducing into the household a man with whom Little Sodbury has been associated ever since. He chose as tutor for his children a

The great hall was built in about 1430. Its proportions are unusual owing to the height of the walls and the steepness of the roof

46

William Tyndale's room,
in which he is supposed
to have begun his translation
of the Bible

brilliant young scholar of both Oxford and Cambridge, already, at the age of twenty-five, distinguished for his learning and piety and for his strong leaning towards the reformed faith. His name was William Tyndale and he arrived at Little Sodbury in 1521, taking up residence in a timber-framed room on the top floor of the newly completed south range. Tradition has it that it was in this room that he began work on his famous translation of the Bible.

Tyndale left the employ of Sir John Walsh in the summer of 1523 to continue his great work, eventually being burnt at the stake for heresy in Flanders in 1536. By a twist of fate his former pupil Maurice Walsh also died by fire, at Little Sodbury, in a bizarre incident recorded by Sir Robert Atkyns in his *Gloucestershire, Past and Present*. 'In the year 1556,' he wrote, 'in less than two months, died Maurice Walsh Esq, together with seven of his children, occasioned by a fiery sulphrous globe rolling in at the parlour door at dinnertime, which struck one dead at the table, and caused the deaths of the rest. It made its passage through a window on the other side of the room.'

In 1608 the Walsh family sold the house to Thomas Stephens, Attorney General to Prince Henry and Prince Charles, later Charles I, who constructed a new staircase to the south of the hall. Further rebuilding took place after the house was extensively damaged by fire during a terrible storm which raged all over England in September 1703, but in the nineteenth century it was all but abandoned, and fell into a sad state of disrepair. Complete collapse was close at hand when, in 1914, it was rescued by Lord Hugh Grosvenor, who gave over the difficult work of restoration to Sir Harold Brakspear, fresh from completing a similar task at Great Chalfield Manor. Today Little Sodbury is virtually as he left it and is the home of its present owners.

A gargoyle in the hall serves as a
squint through which to spy on
the hall from an upper chamber

The cloister. Its function was to connect the screens passage with the pantry, kitchen and buttery, the enormous serving hatch of which can be seen in the foreground

Ockwells Manor

As one proceeds up the drive of Ockwells Manor, formerly the old road from Maidenhead to Windsor, an aura of calm prevails. To the left a magnificent tithe barn, contemporary to the house, borders the original forecourt. Straight ahead the old gatehouse, gabled and timber-framed, marks the entrance to the outer courtyard, while to the right the east façade of the manor is glimpsed through a stand of ancient chestnuts. Timber-framed with brick filling, its appearance is at once striking, both for the large expanse of tiled roof and for its beautiful colour, a combination of the glowing rust of its brickwork, set in a herringbone pattern, and the silvery grey of its oak timbers, many of which are elaborately carved.

It was built between 1446 and 1465 by Sir John Norrys, Master of the Wardrobe to Henry VI. At first sight the early date seems surprising, for at that period most houses of any size were still being built with fortifications. Not so Ockwells, which can justifiably claim to be the earliest surviving example in England of the fully-evolved medieval manor house. It is likely that its architecture was

The great hall is forty feet long, twenty-four feet broad and thirty-six feet high, with an open timber roof with collar-beams, arched braces and one tier of wind-braces. It is unusual for the enormous expanse of glass on the outer side

Armorial glass in the great hall

influenced by other buildings under construction in the area at that date, in particular the collegiate buildings at Eton.

Entering from a wide porch one finds oneself, as one would expect, in the screens passage. Here, however, the house does not quite conform to the standard pattern of the day, that is with chamber and solar to the right of the hall, and kitchen, buttery and pantry to the left, for the latter offices are situated in a separate west range across a small courtyard. The reason for this unusual arrangement may well lie in the fact that the house originally had a chapel which adjoined it at its south-east end, to which it was considered undesirable to have the offices too close. Instead the normal doorways open into two rooms beneath a large chamber which probably served as servants' sleeping quarters.

The hall at Ockwells is by any standards a remarkable room. What raises it into a class of its own is the enormous expanse of glass on the outer side. The upper third of this wall consists of two five-light windows separated only by one of the main verticals of the framing. In the oriel at the high table end of the room there are three window lights in the upper part of the projecting side, and twelve in the main front, thus giving an unbroken sequence of nineteen lights. All of these are of heraldic glass and record the arms of Sir John Norrys' friends and acquaintances at Court.

Perhaps the most unique feature of Ockwells, however, is a complete series of galleries running round three sides of the inner court, both on the ground and first floors. The lower of these, now glazed in, would almost certainly have been an open cloister, but it is the upper of the two which is of special interest. Here we find an exceptionally early example of a communication gallery, the earliest known survival of which is at Eton College. These were virtually unknown in domestic buildings until late in the Elizabethan period. It was primarily this double cloister that inspired Sir Nikolaus Pevsner to call Ockwells 'the most refined and the most sophisticated timber-framed mansion in England.'

The bressumer of the oriel above the entrance porch, finely carved with heraldic emblems

Overleaf: the east front. The house was built between 1446 and 1465 and has a striking appearance owing to the large expanse of tiled roof and the combination of timber-framing and brick filling

53

The screens passage has one of
the earliest fixed screens in the
country. The panels to the right
of the front door are carved with
cinquefoil heads, while those on
the hall side are quite plain.
This suggests that at one time
the whole screen may have
been similarly decorated

The dining room at Ockwells
was probably formerly a
withdrawing room. It has a fine
Elizabethan fireplace and
panelling of the same date, but
retains its original ceiling beams

 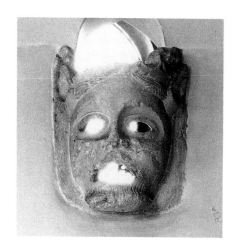 

Squints in the hall: laughing face, king with ass's ears, bishop with mitre

Great Chalfield Manor

I visited Great Chalfield on a hot September morning and was at once captivated by its charm. The approach is a delightful one, down narrow grassy Wiltshire lanes which cut through rolling farmland. A glimpse of stone gables across a meadow, a bend in the road, the glint of water, and there lies before one, quite unexpectedly, a beautiful cluster of buildings, surrounded by a moat, which give the instant impression of having changed little since they were first built. At the centre is the house of locally quarried stone, with a central great hall lit by tall windows, and gables on either side. To the west is the gatehouse with farm buildings beyond; to the east the small parish church of All Saints. It is the perfect English medieval grouping, a reminder of the days when all over England manor house, farm and church were the centre of the community, and this, the north side of the property, has in fact scarcely changed since the fifteenth century. 'It cannot be doubted,' wrote a visitor to Great Chalfield in 1838, 'that the curious and reflecting visitor of Chalfield Manor-House and its appurtenances, will feel his imagination

Instead of an open timber roof, the hall has a slightly cambered plaster ceiling divided into sections by carved wooden beams

58

A topiary house on the large
lawn or 'pleasance'

The north front

somewhat excited, when they carry back his thoughts to the era of their freshness; to the inartificial manners of that early age; and to the scenes of hospitality and merriment, which then gladdened the venerable pile.'

Great Chalfield Manor, one of the few surviving houses of this period in the country, was built between 1465 and 1480 on the site of an earlier fortified house. This had belonged to the Percy family, who had crossed the Channel with William the Conqueror. They held the property from the end of the twelfth century for six generations until it passed by marriage to the Tropnells, a family of modest Wiltshire landowners. Thomas Tropnell, who inherited the property in the 1450s, was a cleverer and more ambitious man than his predecessors. Through shrewd business dealings during the Wars of the Roses, he built up his holding of land to include seven Wiltshire manors. His fortune had increased correspondingly; by the time he became owner of Great Chalfield he was in a position to pull down the old manor and build a house embodying all the latest ideas.

The house is approached from the north, by way of a bridge across the moat. A sharp turn to the left then takes the visitor through the gatehouse to find the fourteenth-century church immediately in front of him, and the house to the right. The house's most striking feature is its symmetry, for one tends to expect the composition of a house of such an early date to be much more haphazard, the architects of the day being usually more concerned with the suitability of a building for defence than with its appearance. Tropnell was evidently a man of vision, for he combined many of the traditional arrangements with an architectural approach far ahead of its time. Thus he retained the idea of a central great hall, lit on both sides and with an independent gable-ended roofline, but at either end he placed identical projecting wings, both with an outer and inner gable, each of the former having a highly enriched and slightly different oriel. This variation, something which would never have been contemplated in the

The ancient gatehouse in the long wing to the north-west of the house

61

A gargoyle on the roof of the
north façade

seventeenth century, is an indication of the intelligent way in which Tropnell was experimenting at a time when there were still no hard and fast rules in architecture. Such freedom is one of the reasons why buildings of this date are so often a source of surprise and delight.

A vaulted porch, within which a corbel to the right of the oak door bears the arms of Thomas Tropnell, leads into the screens passage and thence into the hall. Here another of Tropnell's innovations is to be found, for though the roofline of the hall building, in accord with medieval tradition, would suggest an open timber roof, he chose instead to give the room a slightly cambered plaster ceiling divided into half a dozen panels by huge carved wooden beams. Such a device allowed the space between ceiling and roof to be used as servants' quarters, and staircases at either end permitted access to the rest of the house without traversing the hall. The squints in the hall are extraordinary, each covered by a stone mask hollowed out at the back and with eye and mouth apertures, similar to one at Little Sodbury. There are three of them – a bishop with mitre, a king with ass's ears and a laughing face – making the hall unique in England.

Beyond the screens, between the hall and the kitchen, is another feature which is rare for the period, a separate dining room. This contains a curious mural which may well be a portrait of Tropnell himself, though it seems unlikely that he had five fingers as well as a thumb on each hand! Above this is what would have been one of Tropnell's family rooms, now known as the North Bedroom, which boasts a superb original open timber roof. Much of the rest of the house, however, consists of an extremely sensitive restoration carried out by Sir Harold Brakspear between 1905 and 1912 on behalf of the then owner, Mr Robert Fuller, after the house had fallen into a bad state of disrepair. This was carried out retaining wherever possible the original work. The result is that Great Chalfield has barely altered in appearance since it was built by Thomas Tropnell.

Opposite: the North Bedroom

The former great chamber, now a bedroom, is one of the finest examples of a room of this date in England

Giffords Hall, Wickhambrook

Giffords Hall is not easy to find, lying as it does, quite hidden by trees, at the end of a narrow lane a mile or so off the main road from Bury St Edmunds to Haverhill. The search is well worthwhile however, for there are few more picturesque houses in Suffolk. Unlike its better-known namesake near Stoke-by-Nayland, a semi-fortified building built largely of brick, this house is almost entirely timber-framed and is situated on a moated island accessible by means of a charming triple-arched brick bridge.

Historical evidence points to there having been an earlier house on the site which was replaced c.1480 by the then owner, Clement Higham, who built himself a two-storey house with four rooms on each of the floors, an unusual plan at a time when a central hall with narrow wings at each end was the more normal arrangement. A century later, Clement's great-grandson, Thomas, made further additions, including a second wing on the east side, while a late-Stuart Higham filled in some of the space between the two latter wings in order to produce a new staircase.

The original house was, and still is, entered through a door tucked away on the north side of the two-storey entrance porch which juts out on the west side. This leads into the hall, an extraordinary timber room, lit from both south and west by large transomed windows. Particularly impressive are the enormous upright baulks which support the principal ceiling beams and effectively divide the room into three bays. The hall also contains some lovely linenfold panelling above the chimney-piece, between it and the north wall.

Above the hall is the remarkable great chamber, at present a bedroom, of which it would be hard to find a better example of its date in England. It too is divided into three bays by heavy oak principals, but in this case the beams which they support and which span the room are arched and moulded, as are the purlins which they in turn bear.

The hall, an extraordinary
timber room divided into three
bays by enormous upright
baulks supporting the principal
ceiling beams. The room also
contains some particularly fine
linenfold panelling

66

The dining room is part of a reconstruction carried out in the early part of this century

The cornice is battlemented and there is elaborate carving in the spandrels of the main supports. Of great interest too is the late fifteenth-century Gothic fireplace, with its four-centred arch beneath a battlemented cornice, both ornamented with four-leaf flowers. This was probably imported from elsewhere.

The house fell into disrepair in the eighteenth century and was eventually sold in 1844, only to be converted into workers' tenements. When it was bought by an artist, Mr Seymour Lucas, in 1904, the great chamber was in use as a carpenter's shop. In 1908 he in turn sold it to a Mr Fass, who restored it and built a new north wing in the same style as the rest of the house. It is at present the home of the Gardiner family.

The gatehouse, described by Pugin as 'one of the noblest specimens of domestic architecture of the fifteenth century.' It contains the King's Room on the first floor and the Queen's Room above it

Oxburgh from the north-west. Although it gives the initial impression of being a mighty fort, closer inspection reveals that the fortifications are largely decorative

Oxburgh Hall

Oxburgh, which occurs in the Domesday Book as 'Oxe-burg', meaning the fortified place where oxen are kept, came to the Bedingfield family in the early part of the fifteenth century, through the marriage of Edmund Bedingfield of Bedingfield in Suffolk to Margaret Tuddenham, whose brother, Sir Thomas Tuddenham, had inherited the Norfolk estate from a cousin in 1434. Sir Thomas, whose political intrigues are well documented in the Paston Letters, was executed for treason in 1461 and, having died childless, his lands devolved upon his sister, whose heir was her grandson, Edmund. In 1482, Edward IV granted him permission 'that he according to his will and pleasure may build, make and construct walls and towers with stone, lime and gravel, around and below his manor of Oxburgh in the county of Norfolk, and enclose that manor with walls and towers of this kind; also embattle, crenellate, and machicolate those walls and towers.'

Alec Clifton-Taylor has called the resulting house 'one of England's most enchanting pieces of architectural pageantry.' This is no exaggeration, for though it was built three years before the end of the Wars of the Roses, at a time of great uncertainty and upheaval in England, and has the appearance of a mighty fort, a closer inspection reveals that it is built entirely of brick, a material much too soft to withstand a serious siege, and that its fortifications are largely decorative. Oxburgh is one of those houses which mark the start of the transition of the medieval castle into the comfortable country house.

Augustus Pugin called the gatehouse, a tremendous structure rising sheer from the moat and piercing the north front, 'one of the noblest specimens of domestic architecture of the fifteenth century,' and it is the only part of Oxburgh which remains completely unchanged. On either side of the entrance, octagonal turrets rise up in seven tiers to a height of eighty feet, each topped by double-stepped battlements and furnished with false machicolation. Above the finely-moulded four-centred gateway is a great four-light mullioned window with stepped transoms and arched heads, and above that a similar, if plainer, three-light window. Throughout, the beautiful brickwork is in what is known as 'English bond', alternate courses of 'headers' and 'stretchers' with generous mortar bonds.

Inside, the gatehouse has changed little. Beyond the original massive oak doors the arched entrance has a fine roof divided into rectangular panels by moulded bricks skimmed with plaster. Two little doors on either side of the passageway lead to the porter's lodge on the left, and the armoury on the right, both tall narrow rooms with coved brick ceilings, and it is through a door at the north end of the latter that another of Oxburgh's most interesting architectural features is to be found. This is the circular newel staircase which leads up to the roof. It is made entirely of cut brick, with a moulded brick handrail, and the manner in which the undersides of the steps sweep upwards in one continuous spiral vault leaves one breathless with admiration at the craftsmanship of the Norfolk

The brick newel stair which leads from the armoury up to the King's Room

70

bricklayers of the day. On the first floor, behind the four-light window, is the King's Room, so called because Henry VII lodged there in 1487. Although the ceiling beams and panelling are modern, it remains otherwise the same as when it was built, almost stark in its simplicity, with plain brick walls, a large archway opening into a bay window and a striking brick fireplace with a four-centred arch. The Queen's Room, directly above it, is very similar.

Though the south and west façades of Oxburgh are basically original, if much renewed, the rest of the house has been greatly altered over the centuries. The Reverend Charles Parkin, Rector of Oxburgh in the middle of the eighteenth century, described the main house as it was when he knew it. 'The courtyard (about which stands the house) is 118 feet long and 92 broad; opposite to the great tower on the south side of the court, stands the HALL, in length about 54 feet, and 34 in breadth; between the two bow windows, the roof is of oak, (in the same style and form with that of Westminster) equal in height to the length of it, and being lately very agreeably ornamented and improved may be justly accounted one of the best old Gothick halls in England.' Alas this marvellous room, with its double hammerbeam roof, fell victim to a typical eighteenth-century whim. On 24 April, 1775, Sir Richard Bedingfield noted in his diary: 'Began pulling down ye Old Hall and making the Alterations to ye House.' He demolished the whole of the south range, which included the kitchens and offices, and built instead the saloon, in the south-west corner, for the purpose of housing his collection of pictures.

Carved heraldic emblems set in the brickwork

A squint in the form of a cross
on the gatehouse

One of the quatrefoil windows
giving light to the newel stair

The King's Room. Although the ceiling beams and panelling are modern, this starkly simple room remains otherwise as it was when built

Further alterations were carried out in the nineteenth century by his grandson, Sir Henry Bedingfield who, writing to his brother Felix in 1830, gave his address as 'The Ruin', which suggests that the house had by then fallen into a state of disrepair. He rearranged the interior, creating the present drawing room, library, dining room, billiard room, old kitchen and servants' hall, as well as embellishing the exterior in typical Victorian fashion with Tudor-style windows, tall chimney-stacks and a great tower at the south-east corner.

In spite of the fact that much of the Oxburgh we see today is thus Victorian, the original north front is still the dominating feature and this keeps the medieval atmosphere intact. Bedingfields still occupy part of the house, but only just. In 1951, the family were obliged to sell the property for tax reasons, and soon after it was put up for auction a second time. 'The only prospective buyer,' wrote Nigel Nicolson, 'was a demolition firm that intended to pull it down. On the very morning of the sale, Lady Bedingfield, who had lived here for sixty years, found the necessary money to buy it back. When the name of the purchaser was announced, the audience burst into spontaneous applause.' She subsequently handed it over to the National Trust, in whose hands it has remained.

The east elevation from across the garden

The hall is unusual in that it appears never to have had screens. The entrance door opens directly into it

Cotehele

Cotehele's romantic setting is embodied in its name, a corruption of 'coit hale', meaning a wood on the river. It stands high above the steep banks of the river Tamar, surrounded by woods and looking out over a deep valley across to the viaduct and town of Calstock on the far side of the river. Though its granite walls date from Tudor times, the origins of the house go back to the middle of the fourteenth century, when Hilaria de Cothele, the heiress of the property, married one William Edgecumbe, the second son of Richard Edgecumbe of Endsleigh near Milton Abbott. The house as it stood then was a compact quadrangular fortified building of red sandstone rubble, which still forms the lower courses of the walls which surround the main quadrangle on its south and west sides and parts of its east side. There are also in this inner court some small round-headed windows and a door to the left of the chapel window which are of the same date. The remodelling of the house was the work of Hilaria's descendant, Sir Richard Edgecumbe, a man who is something of a legend in the annals of Cornish history.

Previous page: the gate tower, built by Sir Richard Edgecumbe c.1485, from the outer court. Passing through the archway, a vaulted passage leads into the inner court

In 1483 Edgecumbe, who was M.P. for Tavistock, joined the rebellion against Richard III led by Henry Stafford, Duke of Buckingham, which had been sparked off by the rumour that the King had arranged the murder of the two sons of Edward IV in the Tower of London. The uprising was a disaster, ending with the execution of Buckingham and the outlawing of all those involved. Edgecumbe himself managed to escape and holed up at Cotehele, where he was eventually tracked down by the local agent of the King, Sir Henry Trenowth of Bodrugan, a man detested and feared throughout the county. As Trenowth's troops closed in, however, Edgecumbe gave them the slip, slitting the throat of an unwary sentry and fleeing down the valley to the river, where he employed an ancient device to trick his would-be captors. 'Which extremity,' wrote Richard Carew, the Cornish historian, 'taught him a sudden policy, to put a stone in his cap, and tumble the same into the water, while these rangers were first at his heels, who, looking down after the noise, and seeing his cap swimming thereon, supposed that he had desperately drowned himself, and gave over their further hunting, and left him at liberty to shift away, and ship over into Brittany.'

In Brittany Edgecumbe followed the example of other exiles and joined forces with Henry Tudor. After fighting on Henry's side at the Battle of Bosworth Field in 1485, he was dubbed Knight Banneret and given the post of Comptroller of the King's Household. But his greatest satisfaction came when the King granted to him all the confiscated estates of his old enemy Sir Henry Trenowth, whom he proceeded to hunt down every bit as rigorously as he himself had once been pursued, eventually driving Trenowth to leap to his death from a cliff between Mevagissey and the Dodman, a spot known to this day as Bodrugan's Leap.

Sir Richard Edgecumbe was now a comparatively rich man, and could afford to enlarge and improve the house at Cotehele. He turned it around so that its entrance was

The kitchen

to the south, and set about building a new embattled gateway, a barn and outhouses, a new upper floor all round the court and, as a shrine in memory of his miraculous escape from Sir Henry Trenowth, a chapel with a pinnacled bellcot and priest's room beside it. Sadly, he almost certainly never saw his work completed, since he died in 1489. This was left to his son, Sir Piers Edgecumbe, whose marriage to a great Cornish heiress considerably increased the family fortunes. He could thus afford to add his own contribution to the house in the form of the great hall and the rooms to the south of it, the drawing room on the ground floor and, above it, the solar, now occupied by the South and Red rooms.

It is the great hall which almost all visitors to Cotehele remember best, not for its size, for it is a modest forty feet in length, but for the remarkable way in which the atmosphere of the sixteenth century is preserved within it. It is immediately memorable too for the unusual feature that it appears never to have had screens. Instead of passing in the normal manner through the entrance door into a screens passage, one finds oneself at a stroke within the hall itself, standing upon its cold and sparsely furnished floor of rough stone and cement. The eye is instantly drawn to the ancient uneven whitewashed walls hung from floor to roof by succeeding generations with suits of armour, helmets, breastplates, shields, battle-axes, halberts, pikes, swords, pistols, spears, banners and trophies of the chase. The open timber roof is of an earlier style than might be expected for a hall of this date, being of the medieval type found at houses such as Ockwells, with the spaces between the main purlins being strengthened by intersecting moulded wind-braces.

When William Gilpin, Prebendary of Salisbury, made a voyage up the river Tamar in 1798, he and his companions made a short stop at Cotehele. 'At Cothele house we landed,' he wrote, 'which is entirely surrounded with wood, and shut out from the river. If it were a little opened, it might both see and be seen to advantage. To

The White Room

the river particularly it would present a good object; as it stands on a bold knoll, and is built in the form of a castle. But it is a deserted mansion, and occupied only as a farm house. Here we refreshed ourselves with tea, and larded our bread after the fashion of the country, with clotted cream.' In that both the house and the aspect have barely changed since Gilpin made his visit there, his description might have been written yesterday. Today, however, the house is by no means deserted, though it was precisely this abandonment of Cotehele for many years by the family in favour of Mount Edgecumbe, a larger house they owned in the county, that has preserved it for posterity as arguably the most perfect and authentic Tudor house in Cornwall.

A view from the hall up the main staircase at Cotehele

An oak ceiling-board from an early sixteenth-century four-poster, known as the Cotehele Tester. It was carved in Wales, and bears a Welsh inscription: KYFFARWTH AIGWNA HARRY AP:GR, which roughly translated means: 'An expert was Harry apGriffith who wrought this.'

85

The south front showing the original brick and timber hall house to the left, dominated by one enormous chimney-stack and the former stair turret, now the porch, and the seventeenth-century east wing to the right

Otley Hall

Otley Hall, which lies north of Ipswich on the road to Debenham, is a good example of a manor house built by a typical family of Suffolk squires who rose to prominence in late Tudor England. John Gosnold, M.P. for Ipswich and later Solicitor-General to Edward IV bought the moated manor of Otley in 1450 and built there a two-storey manor hall of the Suffolk L plan. This consisted of the present south wing and the short eastward extension towards the moat. On his death in 1475, his son Robert added a central timbered hall to the north, with a parlour at one end and a service wing beyond the screens passage. Finally, John Gosnold's grandson, also Robert, added a fashionable gallery or banqueting hall to the north of the west end of the original house, overlooking the forecourt and supported on a loggia formed with timber columns. As the fortunes of the staunchly Royalist family collapsed during the Civil War, this is where the building stopped, and today the plan remains much as it was then, although the service wing has long since disappeared and the entrance is now in a different place.

A surviving section of the wall
of Robert Gosnold's gallery,
painted to look like wainscot
and featuring the family coats
of arms

Overleaf: the back of the east
wing from across the moat

The two-storey kitchen and dining hall, converted by the present owners from the earliest part of the house, John Gosnold's south wing

In the sixteenth century, Otley was approached across the north side of the moat, and entered through a door on the far right of the hall. Though the doorway still exists, the main entrance to the house is now on the south side where the original stair turret has been skilfully turned into a porch.

The first room one enters beyond the porch is the hall, a single-storey room with a marvellous oak ceiling divided into four sections by heavy cross and transverse beams which are not only thickly moulded but are crested with a pattern of trefoils. On the south wall is a chimney-piece with a huge bressummer, moulded and crested and extending right along the wall, while at the west end of the hall is the original screen, now open to allow light in from the windows beyond. There is a similar timber ceiling to be found in the parlour, or linenfold room, which opens from the east, formerly the dais, end of the hall, and which is lined with fine oak linenfold wainscot.

Another fascinating survival at Otley is to be found on the first floor of Robert Gosnold's seventeenth-century north-east range. This consisted mainly of a gallery overhanging an open timber loggia, which became known as 'The Plahouse', where sports such as cockfighting and bowls took place. The walls of the gallery were painted to represent wainscot panelling. Some sections of this delightful decoration have happily survived, and are preserved in what is now used as a bedroom.

The entrance front. In the centre
is the fifteenth-century porch, to
the left the battlemented great
hall, while beyond is the early
Tudor south-west wing

Athelhampton Hall

She homed as she came, at the dip of eve
On Athel Coomb
Regaining the Hall she had sworn to leave.
The house was soundless as a tomb,
And she stole to her chamber, there to grieve
Lone, kneeling in the gloom.

Thus did the Dame of Athelhall, the heroine of Thomas
Hardy's poem of the same name, return to her home and a
'loveless bed' after bidding her lover farewell forever.
Hardy, who came from a family of builders, was at one
time apprentice to the architect John Hicks, among whose
commissions was the building of a church at Athelhampton in Dorset. Whilst working on this, Hardy became
fascinated by the history of Athelhampton Hall, the great
house which stood nearby, which he was subsequently to
use as a setting both for the above poem and another, 'The
Children and Sir Nameless', as well as for his macabre
short story, 'The Waiting Supper'.

Athelhampton, one of the finest examples of medieval
domestic architecture in Dorset, stands in a landscape of
water meadows close to the village of Puddletown, its
garden bounded by the river Piddle. 'The veri name intimates nobilitie,' wrote John Coker in his *Survey of Dorsetshire*, no doubt inspired by the local tradition that the
Saxon King Athelstan resided there in the tenth century.
Another Dorset antiquary, John Hutchins, suggested that
the name was derived from that of the renowned Saxon
general Athelhelme, who was killed in action in the year
837 while commanding an army of Dorset men repelling
an invasion of the Danes at Portland. Whatever the truth,
the Saxon origins of the name itself – from 'athel' (noble),
'ham' (home), and 'stan' (denoting the highest degree) –
are evidence enough of the antiquity of the site, the
earliest recorded owners of which were the de Loundres
family, followed, in the reign of Richard II, by the de
Pydeles. It was the marriage of a de Pydele heiress to a Sir

92

Richard Martyn of Waterston in 1350 which began the line whose descendants were to build the house we see today.

Work upon it was started in the reign of Henry VII by Sir William Martyn, a prominent businessman with expanding interests in London, who in 1485 was granted a licence to enclose 180 acres of deer park, and to build a battlemented house with towers. By the time he became Lord Mayor of London, in 1493, that part of his new home which has survived to the present day, namely the embattled hall range which faces the visitor as he approaches from the south, would almost certainly have been completed. It consists of a long two-storey building dominated by a projecting porch, to the left of which stands the hall itself, lit by a fine four-sided oriel and two pairs of arched lights set high up in the wall. Built of creamy limestone ashlar from Portisham, it presents a picturesque sight on a fine day when the sun picks out the dressings of golden Ham Hill stone. To the right of the porch, beyond a later gabled addition, is the service wing, completed by a polygonal turret. The west wing, which forms the north side of the forecourt, was erected by Sir William's son Christopher in the early sixteenth century. Sometime before 1550, his successor, Robert Martyn, added a splendid two-storey gatehouse which adjoined this wing facing the porch, thus creating an inner courtyard. Unfortunately this was demolished in 1862 because it deprived the hall of too much light, though a good idea of its appearance may be had from an illustration in Nash's *Mansions in the Olden Time*.

The great hall itself is generally regarded as one of the finest examples of fifteenth-century domestic architecture in England. On entering, one's eyes are at once drawn upwards to the soaring timbers of its extraordinary open roof, which reaches a height of fifty feet and, though it has been repaired from time to time, remains largely original.

The dovecot has a cedar lantern with landing stages for forty doves and is roofed in eighteenth-century lead, carved with many names including that of Thomas Hardy. There is room inside for 1,500 nests

The modern topiary garden

Its unique features are the unusually large cusps given to
the arch-braces of the principal trusses so that they appear
as a series of bounding trefoil arches. In 'The Waiting
Supper', Thomas Hardy describes the 'braces, purlins and
rafters' as making 'a brown thicket of oak overhead.' The
charming vaulted oriel in the south-west corner, which
forms a connecting passage with the adjoining wing, adds
further character to the room. Its slender three-tier windows, through which the sun streamed on the day I
visited, throwing multi-coloured dappled patterns on
the stone floor, contain some fine tracery and the original
heraldic glass which depicts the various marriage alliances

94

of the Martyn family. In each case this also includes their punning crest of chained ape – 'Martin' being the heraldic name for a monkey – with the motto 'He who looks at Martin's ape, Martin's ape shall look at him.'

A doorway in the oriel leads into an anteroom, the first room in Christopher Martyn's west wing, beyond which lies the great chamber. Though this room and the one above it do contain one or two original features, they are largely reconstructions dating from the latter half of the nineteenth century. This became necessary after the house had fallen into a dreadful state of disrepair under the ownership of the fourth Earl of Mornington, into whose possession it had come in 1812 on his marriage to the great heiress Miss Catherine Tylney-Long. 'Of the miseries which followed this marriage,' noted the Annual Register on his death in 1857, 'and of the subsequent scandals of the deceased's career, it is better to say nothing. The vast property he had acquired by marriage and all that came from his own family was squandered; and, after many years of poverty and profligacy, he subsisted on a weekly pension from his relatives, the late and present Duke of Wellington.' In 1848 Athelhampton was sold to a Mr George Wood, under whose ownership its decline continued. He pulled down the gatehouse and generally neglected the whole property, so that by the time it changed hands again, bought by Mr Alfred de Lafontaine in 1891, the hall was 'in utter wretchedness. The roof blanched with mildew . . . Outside the earth rose above the floor level so that at time water stood on the dank flags.' He began a programme of restoration which has been continued by the present owners, the Cooke family, with the result that Athelhampton remains essentially medieval, surrounded by walls and courts, much as in former days.

The great chamber has a seventeenth-century ceiling and panelling

Opposite: the great hall, whose timbered roof remains substantially as it was when it was built, before 1500. Much of the heraldic glass in the windows also dates from this time

A view through to the chapel adjoining the state bedroom

Two of the doors in the Council Chamber. The one on the left leads up past a priest's hole to a room known as the Priest's Room

Compton Wynyates, known as 'Compton-in-the-Hole' since it lies in a hollow, with low hills rising on all sides

Compton Wynyates

Compton Wynyates is said by many to be the most perfect Tudor house in England. 'No one can see it and remain unmoved,' wrote William, Marquis of Northampton at the turn of the century: 'One is carried away from this world and into some other where the supernatural would be quite at home, and where anything trivial or modern or practical would be out of place.' He might be said to have been biased, since he lived there, but my initial glimpse of the house, of the south and west fronts through a gap in the trees, proved him right, for it was a sight that literally took my breath away.

Compton Wynyates lies cradled in a hollow, at the foot of gently wooded grassy hills which rise away from it on all sides. It is built of brick whose age gives it its beautiful variation of colour – shades of pink, russet, plum, red, which change dramatically with the light. A diaper pattern on the walls is created by the use of bricks of a peculiar bluish colour attributed to the fumes of the burning wood in the kiln. The architecture is equally irregular, which is undoubtedly part of Compton's charm. Though basically a

Overleaf: the west front at dusk

The Big Hall rises
to the full height of the house
and has a finely moulded
timber roof

The Royal Arms of Henry VIII,
carved above the entrance porch

foursquare house round a courtyard, it rambles in zig-zag fashion with clusters of crenellated towers of unequal height jostling for position with gables, some half-timbered, the whole bristling with elaborate brick chimneys of different designs.

In the early part of the thirteenth century, when one Philip de Compton was lord of the manor, there was a house on the site which was demolished by his descendant Edmund de Compton in the latter half of the fifteenth century. He then set about the construction, on the same moated site, of a new building, probably a simple square structure in the style of Ightham Mote. His son William, who succeeded in 1493, was page to the future King Henry VIII, on whose succession he was appointed First Gentleman of the Bedchamber, a post of considerable importance. He soon set about the embellishment of his family home, and it was he who left behind him the house we see today.

One enters Compton Wynyates through a yawning embattled porch, once an entry for horsemen who would have crossed the now filled-in moat by means of a drawbridge whose chains have left deep grooves above the arch. Passing through, one is left in no doubt as to the loyalty of the builder to his monarch, for there above are emblazoned the Royal Arms supported by a dragon and a greyhound and surmounted by a crown around which runs the inscription 'DOM REX HENRICUS OCTAV'. A charming courtyard lies within, dominated by the great oriel window of the hall. The Big Hall, as it is called, is the first room entered beyond the screens passage. It has a finely moulded open timber roof which springs from a richly carved cornice and is thought to have come from the fifteenth-century castle of Fulbrooke, which King Henry had given as a gift to William Compton. That it was originally made for a larger place is evident from the fact that the wall-posts are cut off in irregular lengths and do not rest on corbels as they rightly should. Another feature of the Big Hall is the screen with its fine carving, including a central panel depicting the battle of Tournai in 1512 in

The Council Chamber, whose
walls are covered with wainscot
boards of split oak, and which
has the unusual distinction of
having six doors

The Priest's Room. Sloping
timbers with plaster between
them form the walls, and
beneath the south-west window
is a large slab of elm thought to
have been used as an altar

The hall
oriel from
the inner
court

which William fought alongside his monarch, and linen-fold panels, above which rise the half-timbered walls of the minstrels' gallery.

Apart from a Victorian staircase which leads from the Big Hall up to the drawing room on the first floor, Compton Wynyates remains essentially the house that William Compton built, and in no rooms does one get a stronger sense of a romantic past than in those in the south-west tower. Having climbed the massive circular oak staircase one finds oneself in the 'Council Chamber'. In this extraordinary room there are no fewer than six doors, two giving access to newel staircases, one of which leads past a priest's hole to a room in the roof known as the Priest's Room, which tradition says was used as a Romish chapel in the days of persecution. Here three more doors, with newel staircases also leading away from them, are a further reminder of the dangers of the times.

That Compton Wynyates has survived so remarkably intact is perhaps due to a collapse of the family fortunes in the latter half of the eighteenth century. Spencer Compton, eighth Earl of Northampton, came close to bringing about its total destruction. Having bankrupted himself through gambling and fighting a recklessly extravagant Parliamentary election in 1768, he fled to Switzerland, from where he issued orders for the demolition of Compton Wynyates since he could no longer afford to keep it up. Luckily his faithful steward, John Birrell, who loved the house as if it were his own, chose to ignore these instructions. Instead he blocked up most of the windows to avoid the window tax, disposed of the contents by sale, and kept the place patched up for posterity as best he could. For the better part of a century the house lay empty, thus almost entirely escaping the major alterations that so often took place under the Georgians and Victorians. Poverty and neglect proved a blessing in disguise, preserving the atmosphere of absolute timelessness which still exists at Compton Wynyates today.

A curious carved detail of a small man climbing up a stone drainpipe

The east and north sides of Helmingham, with the east bridge reflected in the moat

Helmingham Hall

Helmingham, for over five hundred years the home of the Tollemache family, is one of the most romantic houses in England. The approach up its drive is an exciting one, for the house, raised up on a slight summit and at first hidden by trees, suddenly comes into full view, its crow-stepped gables and clusters of Tudor chimneys silhouetted against the sky. The moat, however, cannot be seen until one is at its very edge, when it is dramatically revealed that Helmingham sits in the middle of an island and is accessible only by means of a drawbridge.

Helmingham came to the Tollemaches through marriage when, in 1487, John Tollemache of Bentley, south of Ipswich, a prominent local squire, married Elizabeth Joyce, the widow of William Joyce of Helmingham, and came to live with her in a house then called Creke's Hall, after the family who had possessed it in early Plantagenet times. John Tollemache then assured his family's succession to the Creke's Hall manor by arranging the marriage of his son from a previous marriage, Lionel, to the Joyce heiress, and it was he who, on his father's death in 1510,

The hall is one of the few rooms in Helmingham to have kept something of its original appearance. It retains its plan and some of the fifteenth-century roof timbers

set about the extensive rebuilding of the existing structure and the creation of what was effectively a new house on the site.

Retaining the hall range of William Joyce's building, and the entrance gate which must have existed to the south of it, Tollemache built a quadrangular gabled house, largely of close-set timber-framing. Some of the latter can still be seen on the west wall of the entrance gateway. In spite of numerous alterations down the years, the Helmingham we see today still preserves the original plan. Having crossed the moat, one enters through a two-storey brick gateway with diagonal buttresses, which is for the most part Tudor. Beyond the entrance is the hall range, with a porch which opens into the east end of the hall itself. The west range, to the left of the hall, contains all the best rooms and was the main residential wing, while the east range was and still is the kitchen wing.

In the course of the seventeenth century a series of judicious marriages brought the owners of Helmingham great estates in Northamptonshire and Cheshire, Ham House and the Earldom of Dysart. It was Lionel, fourth Earl of Dysart, who made the first major changes to the house in about 1750; he faced the timber-framed walls with brick and weather tiles and inserted sash windows.

In 1800 the sixth Earl called in John Nash and his assistant John Repton to give a Gothic treatment to Helmingham. This included the replacement of the original mullioned windows, and the addition of buttresses, finials and battlements in the Tudor style. Nash also chose to cover the exterior with a coating of cement to give the effect of masonry. Luckily for posterity, as J. P. Neale tells us in his *Views of Seats*, the Earl's sister, Louisa, Countess of Dysart, who succeeded him in 1821, 'very judiciously removed' this. Finally, in 1840, John, first Lord Tollemache, called in Anthony Salvin to remodel the west front. This was carried out in a richly revivalist Tudor style, all the details being carefully copied from the original features on the entrance front.

The massive sixteenth-century kitchen is still in use

The exterior of Compton Castle has not been altered since the early sixteenth century. It thus retains almost the exact appearance it would have had in the reign of Henry VIII

Compton Castle

The land on which Compton Castle stands has been owned by the Gilbert family, with a single break, from the early fourteenth century to the present day. Sometime between 1311 and 1329 the Gilberts built a conventional medieval manor house on the site. Between 1450 and 1475 the buildings at the west end of the hall, the solar and a cellar were pulled down and rebuilt on a much larger scale.

The third and final stage in the building of Compton Castle was carried out in 1520, with the addition of the striking fortifications which give Compton such an air of romance.

By the middle of the eighteenth century the Gilbert family had made another property their main home, and the old house fell into disrepair. In 1785 they sold the house, and when Burke visited it early in the nineteenth century he described it as 'a ruined pile'. It was in this condition that Walter Gilbert saw the house in 1904 and vowed that one day he would buy it back into the family. He was able to do so in 1930. A slow and painstaking programme of restoration followed, and in 1951 he handed the property over to the National Trust.

The great kitchen dates from c.1520. It has a hearth which extends its whole width, and its chimney is divided into three flues to give support to the inside wall and to improve the draught

The east front, the crowning glory of which is the great semi-octagonal oriel, rising to the full height of the building

Horham Hall

Horham Hall, one of the finest pre-Reformation brick houses in Essex, lies halfway between Thaxted and Broxted, straddling the parish boundary which actually runs through the entrance porch and the great hall. This almost certainly explains the origin of its name, which derives from the Saxon words 'ora', meaning a border, and 'ham', meaning a dwelling place. The antiquary John Leland described Horham when he made a trip to East Anglia in the 1530s and noted 'Old Cutte builded Hore-ham Haule, a very sumptuous house in Estfex by Thax-stede, and there is a goodly pond or lake by it and faire parkes thereabouts.'

The 'Old Cutte' to whom Leland referred was Sir John Cutte, Under Treasurer to Henry VIII, who bought the Horham estate, where there then stood a timber-framed house built c.1470 by one Richard Large, in 1502. Rather than demolish this, Cutte included it in his rebuilding

The great hall rises the full height of the house and retains its coved and panelled ceiling. This has a central louvre to provide access to a charming lantern on the roof

The north elevation from across
the moat

plans, extending his new home to the north and turning part of the old building, including the solar, into his domestic offices. The house he built was on the traditional H plan, with the east entrance front we see today in the centre, and flanking wings running down to the moat, linked by a gatehouse. Though part of the wings and the gatehouse have since disappeared, the east façade, built of red brick with stone dressings and some blue diapering, remains little changed. It is delightfully irregular, the contour broken by gables, crenellations and chimney-stacks of different heights, while the varying shades of the brickwork, which change constantly with the light, give it an almost magical quality. But the crowning glory of the front is undoubtedly the great semi-octagonal hall oriel, rising to the full height of the building, with its four rows of lights, individually arched and cusped, and a glazed frieze of quatrefoils along the top.

At the south end of this entrance front, a two-storey porch leads through a four-centred outer archway into the screens passage, to the left of which are the three doors which once led to the buttery, kitchen and pantry of Richard Large's fifteenth-century house. Passing through into this south wing, one can see that some of his building still survives. In one corner of what is now the dining room, for example, one of the original oak wallposts has been uncovered. Attached to it is a shaft with a moulded capital and a curved bracket which indicate that the Large house was half-timbered with a projecting upper storey. More dramatic, however, is the solar, above this room on the first floor, which has a beautiful and richly moulded open timber roof with king-post, tie-beams and curved wind-braces.

The great hall is the showpiece of Cutte's house, retaining its original coved and panelled ceiling. At all times of day this hall is filled with a beautiful soft light which comes from the huge oriel with its forty lights. An archway at the north-east end of the hall probably once led to a chapel which was started by John Cutte, who died before

The semi-octagonal oriel is among the grandest to be found in a house of this size. It has four rows of lights and a glazed frieze of quatrefoils along the top

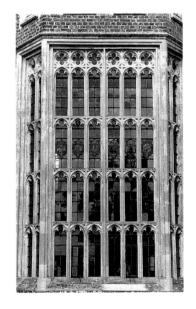

117

The screens passage with three doors on the left which once led to the buttery, kitchen and pantry of Richard Large's fifteenth-century house

it was completed, specifying in his will that he was 'to be buried in the parish church of Thaxted until such time as this chapel be fully builded.'

After Sir John Cutte's death in 1520, he was succeeded first by a son who died four years later, and then by a grandson who also died early. It was the son of the latter, another Sir John Cutte, who was the next member of the family to leave his mark on Horham. He it was who built the prominent staircase tower which rises up on the right as one looks at the east front, for the purpose, so it is thought, of enabling Queen Elizabeth to watch hawking in the park. The Queen and her court are known to have made two visits to Horham. The first was in 1571, when she stayed for nine days. Her second visit was in 1578, on which occasion she received the envoy of the Duke of

Anjou who was seeking her hand in marriage. The room which she occupied on these occasions, known somewhat unsurprisingly as Queen Elizabeth's Room, is on the first floor of the north wing and has a barrel-vaulted ceiling with moulded ribs.

Perhaps the reason Elizabeth I liked to stay with Sir John can be surmised from an anecdote related by Fuller, who tells of how Her Majesty once sent a certain Spanish Ambassador to stay with 'Old Cutte': 'The Ambassador coming hither, and understanding his name to be John Cuts, conceived himself disparaged to be sent to one of so short a name; the Spanish gentlemen generally having such voluminous surnames, usually adding the place of their habitation for the elongation thereof. But, soon after, the Don found that what the Knight lacked in length of name, he made up in largeness of entertainment.' Such was his extravagance, in fact, that he was eventually obliged to sell Horham in 1599 and move to another house he owned at Childerley in Cambridgeshire. Horham was bought shortly afterwards by Sir William Smith, nephew of Sir Thomas Smith, scholar and Secretary of State to Edward VI and Elizabeth, and became a second residence of the Smith family who owned it till the middle of the nineteenth century. It is due to their lack of interest in it that it escaped the alterations that were the ruination of so many of these early houses in the eighteenth and nineteenth centuries and has thus remained a valuable survival.

The solar, now in use as a bedroom, dates from c.1470, and has recently been restored to its original form

The south front of Giffords Hall

Giffords Hall, Stoke-by-Nayland

Giffords Hall lies in unspoiled Suffolk farmland watered by three rivers, the Brett, the Box and the Stow. There was a Robert Mannock in Stoke-by-Nayland in the reign of Edward III, and it was his grandson, Philip, who bought the local estate of Giffords and established a line there which was to last till the late nineteenth century. Though the name of Giffords Hall comes from a Peter Gifford who held the manor in 1272, the building we see today is the work of the Mannock family. It does possibly incorporate, however, the remains of an earlier house, built either by Gifford or by his predecessor, Richard Constable, who is known to have built the thirteenth-century chapel which lies in ruins opposite the gatehouse.

The first view of the house is of the south front, a long low building, part brick, part flint, part half-timbered, pierced by a gatehouse leading through into a courtyard. The gatehouse which was probably begun c.1520, by George Mannock, grandson of Philip, is of rose-coloured

The inner courtyard with the gatehouse on the left

120

The hall ceiling is of the double hammerbeam type, with five great free-flying trusses, and is memorable for the delightful carvings in the spandrels of the arched braces

brick. It is a modest affair of two storeys, with ribbed polygonal towers and a wide four-centred arch, its turrets raised well above the body of the building. One only notices its considerable width when one passes through into the inner courtyard and turns around to find that the embattled gatehouse has turned into a charming two-storey building with arched windows, topped by a crow-stepped parapet with pyramidal finials.

The great depth of the gatehouse rendered it necessary to divide it into two sections by means of a central arch hung with massive oak doors. Beyond these lies the inner quadrangle, to the south-west and west of which is a half-timbered range. Directly opposite, on the north side, is the hall range, dominated by a big brick porch with a timber-framed upper storey. The latter is a late-Victorian copy of the porch of the Guildhall at Lavenham, ten miles to the north.

It is the early sixteenth-century hall which is the glory of Giffords. There are few such magnificent timber roofs in all England. Among its most memorable features are the delightful carvings in the spandrels of the arched braces, something not uncommon in churches, but rare in domestic architecture. At the east end of the hall is a gallery of the late seventeenth century, which has twisted balusters, and a staircase of c.1630 leading up to it.

The Mannock family occupied Giffords till the latter half of the nineteenth century, when it fell into disrepair. When it was visited in 1883 by the Suffolk Archaeological Society, they found it 'in a sorry condition owing to want of use.' Luckily it was soon after sold to a Mr Brittain who rescued the house from what would have been a sad fate, and since the 1930s it has been the home of the Brockle-bank family.

The entrance front. The west wing to the left comprises work carried out c.1480 and c.1518, while the south, central block and staircase turret dates from c.1616

Westwood Manor

Westwood is situated upon the beautiful high land which lies between the valleys of the Avon and the Frome, on the extreme western edge of Wiltshire, two miles from Bradford-on-Avon and eight miles from Bath. As early as 1400 there seems to have existed some kind of structure there. It was probably of two storeys and stood at the south end of the west wing of the present house, built as a home either for the local priest or for the farmer who then held the land. The foundation of the present house was laid in 1480 when Thomas Culverhouse, a successful farmer, owned the property and carried out an extensive programme of building.

The next period of building activity began about 1518 when Westwood benefited from the fortune of a new owner, a prosperous West Country clothier called Thomas Horton. He enlarged Culverhouse's central block and joined it to the earlier building to the west, thus creating a continuous range. His two best rooms were the solar, at present the sitting room, and the panelled room above it. A long east wing, running parallel to the west wing and

The Corner Room is entirely the work of John Farewell. The scallop shells which appear on his arms in the great parlour are also seen on the ceiling here

124

giving the house an H shape, may also have existed at this period, as well as two rear wings to the north and west.

The final stage in the evolution of Westwood Manor took place in the early seventeenth century when the then resident, Toby Horton, sold the house to his brother-in-law, John Farewell. Farewell moved in in 1616 and almost immediately made considerable alterations. He demolished the two rear wings and the long east wing, erecting in place of the latter a small wing at the east corner which continued the line of the main building. Much of the interior was also remodelled. The two-storey hall, for example, was divided into two, with new windows, a screen and a finely carved archway being introduced into the lower half. The top half he converted into the great parlour, which is certainly the most beautiful room in the house, with its fine shallow coved plaster ceiling and lovely views out across the forecourt. The plasterwork is of high quality, with elaborately carved trails of acanthus leaves and other floral patterns.

The Farewell family owned Westwood until the early eighteenth century, after which there was a decline in its fortunes and it became little more than a farmhouse. When it was eventually bought in 1911 by a Mr Edward Lister, the great parlour, for example, had been divided into two with one half being used as an apple store. Lister, a man of considerable taste, set about a sensitive programme of restoration, creating a home for himself which was a perfect evocation of the past. 'Each time I come here,' wrote James Lees-Milne in August 1942, 'I am overwhelmed by the perfection of this house.' Lees-Milne was visiting the house to discuss Lister's request that the National Trust should take it over after his death. They are now its guardians.

The great parlour has a coved ceiling elaborately carved with acanthus leaves and other floral designs

The east front, with the chapter house to the right, now used by the family as a chapel, the parlour, now used as a dining room, in the centre, and the calefactory on the left

Beeleigh Abbey

Less than a mile to the west of the ancient town of Maldon, which stands on a hill above it, and close to the banks of the river Chelmer, lies Beeleigh Abbey. Dedicated to St Nicholas and St Mary, it was, in medieval times, a place of great importance, a house of the order of Premonstratensian or White Canons. All that now remains, however, of the twelfth- and thirteenth-century buildings are parts of the east and south ranges flanking the cloisters. These include the chapter house and first-floor dormitory with its undercroft in the east range, and a passage and room at the north end of the south range, the two groups of buildings being linked by a picturesque three-storey annexe, timber-framed and gabled, erected soon after the dissolution of the Abbey in 1536.

Approaching from the south-west, the initial view of Beeleigh gives no clue as to its ecclesiastical nature. The tall sixteenth-century timber-framed addition with its steeply pitched roof gives the building the appearance of an Elizabethan manor house rather than of a medieval monastery. It comes as something of a surprise, therefore,

The Tudor west wing

The calefactory, once
the monks' dining room and now
in use as a sitting room

when, on entering the house, one finds oneself almost
immediately descending into a dramatic vaulted undercroft. This, the calefactory, was the monks' dining room,
and is used by the present owners, Christina Foyle and
her husband, as their main sitting room. It is divided into
four bays by a central arcade of circular columns of Purbeck marble which have moulded bases and bell-capitals.
In the west wall is a huge fireplace surrounded by a carved
stone frieze of six angels holding musical instruments,
under an enriched and embattled cornice, part of the
canopy of the tomb of the Abbey's patron, Henry
Bourchier, Earl of Essex. The room is lit by three fifteenth-
century windows, each of three cinquefoiled and
transomed lights with vertical tracery under a four-centred
head. The stained-glass panels, depicting the life of the
Virgin Mary, are the original windows from Beeleigh and
were found stored in Westminster Abbey.

The former monks' dormitory, now the library

On the north side of the calefactory, a barrel-vaulted parlour, now in use as a dining room, whose walls bear traces of thirteenth-century wall paintings done by the monks, leads to the chapter house. Built c.1225, this consists of two ranges of four bays divided by a row of three Purbeck marble octagonal columns, each with moulded capital and base supporting quadripartite vaulting. The light comes from lancet windows on all sides, and in the west wall, between two thirteenth-century windows, is a double entrance of the same date with moulded two-centred arches. The chapter house is now used by the family as a private chapel for weddings and christenings, and for occasional Sunday services in the summer, when the sound of hymns floating across the lawn on the evening air serves as a reminder of Beeleigh's religious origins.

From the south end of the calefactory, steps lead to the Tudor wing. On the ground floor is a small, heavily-timbered drawing room, and above are various rooms in use as bedrooms, one of which has an especially good timber roof and an elaborate bed built for James I. But the glory of Beeleigh is the room which runs the length of the space above the calefactory. This, the former dormitory, was originally L-shaped, extending over the whole of the calefactory, the parlour and the chapter house. The north end, over the chapter house, has since been rebuilt, while the south end was partitioned off in the sixteenth century and subdivided into two storeys, with a dog-legged staircase in the western half. It has as its main feature a most beautiful waggon roof, with double collar-beams and trussed rafters supported by arched braces, all made of chestnut. From the sixteenth-century windows along the east wall there are lovely views across the Essex marches. The room is now a library, housing Mr Foyle's famous collection of manuscripts and rare books.

Those lucky enough to visit Beeleigh Abbey could never come away disappointed, partly because the owners' enthusiasm for the place is quite infectious. 'The Abbey really is one of the loveliest homes in England,' writes Miss Foyle. 'Every room is beautiful and the prospect from each window gives delight. Some look over lawns where peacocks strut, others to the river and the marshes, but everywhere it is peaceful and serene . . . We have cared for Beeleigh Abbey for more than forty years, looking upon it as a sacred trust, and it is my dearest wish that whoever follows us here will feel as we do about this lovely and hallowed place.'

A bedroom in the Tudor wing.
The bed was made for James I

The hall. The window high up to the right of the fireplace still contains its original glazing

Beckley Park

Beckley Park stands on the edge of Otmoor, a strange and remote area of marshland that is little known even to the inhabitants of Oxford, a mere six miles to the north-east. In spite of its closeness to the city, it is still comparatively inaccessible, reached only by a circuitous by-road which skirts the moor via the seven villages of Beckley, Fencott, Murcott, Charlton, Oddington, Noke and Islip, for which, in bygone days, it once served as common pasture ground. The site is an ancient one, first achieving importance as early as the time of King Alfred, in whose will it is mentioned as Beccaule.

Then some kind of castle surrounded by a moat probably existed here, guarding the Roman road that ran from Dorchester to Alcester. After the Conquest, the land passed through the hands of various powerful Norman barons. In 1227 it was conferred by Henry III on his brother Richard, Earl of Cornwall, who was the only Englishman ever to be elected Holy Roman Emperor. He

The north elevation with its three projecting gables which accommodate the garderobe flues. The centre gable also contains a newel staircase

136

The former buttery, once used for the storage of ale and still in service as a room in which to prepare drinks

A detail of the buttery

The underside of the newel stair

stocked the park with deer and built a hunting lodge. He also added a further two moats to the one which already existed. The house we see today stands on the narrow strip of ground between the inner and middle moats. It was built in about 1540 by Sir John, later Lord Williams of Thame. It is chiefly of brick but incorporates some stone from the original building which had been given to him by Henry VIII, and which was by then in ruins. Since that date it has changed remarkably little.

Beckley is hard to find, at the end of a long, rough track crossing flat fenland where the brood mares of the Black Prince once roamed. After a mile or so, one rounds a bend to find a tall, narrow house, three stories high and one room wide, standing in the middle of a rectangular moat. The brick is the colour of ripe plums, picked out in diamond ornamental work with black headers. The south-facing façade, with its stone-dressed windows, is approached across the middle moat by a double-arched stone bridge contemporary with the house, and is pretty enough, but the true architectural beauty of Beckley is to be found at its rear where three projecting gables soar dramatically upwards. These accommodate the garderobe flues which would have been necessary for a lodge such as this which, during the hunting season, would have had to accommodate many guests. The whole presents a beautiful contrast in colour to the different greens of the box and yew topiary garden which surrounds it.

The house is cool and dark and shafts of sunlight pierce the shadows. The arrangement is the normal one for a house of this date with its hall, parlour, buttery and kitchen. The hall is a well-furnished and comfortable room with Turkish rugs on the stone floor. It is sixteen feet wide, which is the total width of the house, and twenty-two feet long, lit by two large windows, one of which, high up and to the right of the fireplace, still retains its early seventeenth-century glazing. At its eastern end, where the screens passage once ran, a sturdy double-leaved door leads into the old buttery. Unusually, the posts at the

The door leading from the Oak
Room into the garden

bottom of the doorframe have at some time been scooped
away, presumably to allow for the massive casks which
would have had to pass through it. Beyond the buttery lies
the old kitchen, now in use as a dining room, which still
retains the huge original fireplace with the remains of a
device for turning spits by means of the hot air passing up
the chimney.

At the other end of the hall is the former parlour, now
known as the Oak Room, which has fine Jacobean panelling. 'In winter,' remembers a daughter of the family, 'the
house was so cold that nobody came near us. When my
hot-water bottle fell out of bed it was frozen in the morning. We lived in our overcoats. The oak room was kept
warm, and from there we would make a run for the
kitchen. I remember the cosiness of the winter evenings,
when the wind raged outside, sitting huddled in front of
the big fire, with one of my parents reading. With the wind,
and the trickle of water falling from the outer moat into the
inner one, the outside world seemed very far away.'

Opposite the entrance into the hall lies the only staircase
in the house, a perfect newel stair of solid oak so hard that
the steps have survived 450 years with scarcely a blemish.
This leads to the upper floors; on the first are two curiosi-
ties. One is what is now the door to the main bedroom.
Dating back to 1540, it is of an elaborate design of delicate
linenfold panelling. The other is a delightful north-facing
casement window in the east bedroom which has a
wooden frame set into it, within which is hinged another
frame containing a shutter and grooved for the reception
of glazing.

At the top of the stairs, beyond a lovely oak lattice-work
balustrade, also dating back to 1540, is the attic, a long
dark gallery lit only by the windows in one of the projecting gables. From here there is a breathtaking view over the
yew and rose gardens to the flat and desolate meadows of
Otmoor, a view which has changed little over the centuries. The memory of it cannot fail to linger in the minds
of all those who visit this extraordinary house.

The old kitchen, now the dining
room, still retains the huge
ancient fireplace with the
remains of a device for turning
spits by means of hot air passing
up the chimney

The north front of Collacombe
with the Tamar Valley beyond

Collacombe Manor

'The pleasure of a visit to Collacombe,' wrote Rachel
Evans in her book *Tavistock and its Vicinity*, published in
the latter half of the nineteenth century, 'will well repay
the trouble of a lengthened walk. I was delighted many
summers since by spending an afternoon in rambling
about this ruined mansion. Our young hostess gave us
leave to wander at will among the crumbling staircases
and desolate apartments; so we scrambled up the broad
stairs, and found our way into a place, then used as a wool-
chamber, but evidently a handsome withdrawing-room in
former years.'

This ancient home of the Tremayne family is as well
worth a visit today as it was when Rachel Evans visited it
in 1846. Situated in remote country between the villages of
Lamerton and Sydenham Damerel to the north-west of
Tavistock, it is a striking sight when one first comes across
it at the end of a narrow lane and through a farmyard. A
massive stone wall, pierced with musket embrasures, con-
ceals a substantial L-shaped manor house of grey Devon-
ian slate. The east wing, to the left of the main block, was

The unusual Renaissance
gateway which pierces the
massive wall of the forecourt

143

built early in the fifteenth century, possibly by a Thomas Tremayne or his son Nicholas. The north-facing central block dates from the middle of the sixteenth century and was almost certainly begun by Thomas' son, Roger.

One gets a clue that there might be something rather out of the ordinary within from the archway in the centre of the wall which, though typical of the date in the flat curve of the arch, is contained within Tuscan columns. The porch of the house itself has similar columns and a Palladian-style pediment. These Renaissance touches are continued to an even greater degree in the great hall. The lunette scallops, for example, which surmount the three windows high in the south wall, are a typical Italian motif. Of the extraordinary overmantel containing the Tremayne arms, Christopher Hussey wrote 'The design . . . is of a stylishness not seen again till Inigo Jones designed the Queen's House forty years later. Serlio, the earliest edition of whose book could have been known to Tremayne, affords no prototype for it, which raises the wild surmise that it is a recollection of one by Palladio himself seen in Venice or Vicenza.' The Tremayne in question, who carried out the additional work to the hall in 1574, was Edward, who inherited Collacombe in 1572.

Collacombe has been much changed both internally and externally over the years. The house almost certainly had another storey with a gallery running the length of the central range, this and the west wing being demolished in the early nineteenth century when the Tremaynes sold Collacombe. It subsequently fell into the sad condition in which it was found by Rachel Evans.

Thus the house remained until 1948 when a new owner, Major Jack, began to restore it. Visitors to the house today can see, apart from the hall, various early details such as the early Tudor staircase to the east of the hall, one or two original fireplaces, and 'two full-length figures' which Rachel Evans had seen in the 'wool-chamber', and which now decorate the sixteenth-century fireplace in a small sitting room in the east wing.

An exterior view of the remarkable eighteen-light oriel, which still retains its original glazing of 3,400 panes

The great hall. Its original ceiling and plasterwork of 1574 is full of Italianate detail, such as the lunette scallops surmounting the three windows high in the south wall

145

The north front has a symmetry unusual for its early date

Poundisford Park

Poundisford Park was built by William Hill in 1546. On his return from a trading mission to the Guinea Coast of Africa, he found that his younger brother was already building a house on land which by rights should have been his. Undaunted, he approached the owner of the neighbouring estate, somehow persuaded him to part with his lease, and at once set about building there 'as good a house or better as quickly'. The result is especially interesting architecturally in that it shows how in the last years of the reign of Henry VIII, the medieval concept of the plan of a house governing its appearance was beginning to disappear in favour of a new desire for symmetry.

While the exterior of the house illustrates the transition between early and late Tudor design, the interior is pure Elizabethan and later. The most interesting room is the hall, which was altered by William Hill c.1570. It has a fine plaster ceiling in the Gothic style with a design of spidery ribs forming star and lozenge patterns and issuing from a series of pendants.

The hall. A curiosity is the screen which, instead of supporting a gallery open to the main room, is topped by a cove carrying a plaster partition which effectively closes the gallery off

The Court of the Sovreigns, built by Robert Haydon sometime after 1587. The four statues of Henry VIII, Edward VI, Mary and Elizabeth I are from 1617, the date appearing under the niche which shelters the figure of Elizabeth

Cadhay

The enchanting Tudor manor house of Cadhay is set in a landscape of peaceful farmland and meadows to the north-west of Ottery St Mary. An avenue of limes, to the south of the road from Ottery to Talaton, borders the drive which leads up to the rather dull north front, whose stepped gables, sliding sash windows and pedimented front door seem to suggest a house of the late seventeenth century. A quick look at the east front, however, with its mullioned windows, symmetrically projecting bays and central polygonal stair turret, soon reveals Cadhay's true origins.

The builder of Cadhay was a successful London lawyer named John Haydon. 'He obtained from King Henry VIII,' recorded John Prince in *The Worthies of Devon*, 'a charter for incorporating the Parish of Saint Mary Ottery, in the county, and was first the governor of that corporation himself . . . He procured that King's Letters Patent for the founding a grammar school in that town also; and was very instrumental in getting it well endow'd . . .' Cadhay itself came into his possession through his marriage to

Joan Grenville, the only daughter of the last of the de Cadehaye family, who had owned the land since the reign of Edward I, and had given their name to the hall house which they built there about 1420. When the collegiate foundation of Ottery St Mary was dissolved in 1545, Haydon used his influence to buy up much of the fabric and used the stone to rebuild this house.

The house which Haydon built formed three sides of a square, with the main entrance on the north front and an open prospect to the south. The general appearance would have been very similar to that of the east front as it stands today. The fabric was mainly of Salcombe sandstone with stone dressings from the quarry of Beer, which supplied the stone for the building of Exeter Cathedral. The main room was the hall, on the north side, which rose up through two stories to an open timber roof. To the west was a service wing containing the kitchen and servants' quarters; to the east the family wing with withdrawing rooms on the ground floor and sleeping apartments above, reached by the circular stair in the turret.

Henry VIII

Elizabeth I

The south and east fronts.
The latter, with its mullioned
windows, symmetrically
projecting bays and central stair
turret, shows the style of the
house built by John Haydon
between 1546 and 1550.

The south front from across
the ancient fishponds

When John Haydon died in 1587, Cadhay passed to his great-nephew, Robert, and it was he who gave the house its most memorable feature. He filled in the open south side by building a long gallery of unusually simple design for a period when ornate decoration and plasterwork were customary. He made up for the lack of embellishment in this room, however, by his treatment of the inner court. Here the walls were patterned in a dramatic fashion with an irregular chequering of sandstone and flint. Above each central doorway he inserted deep niches with elaborate Renaissance surrounds into which were placed statues of Henry VIII and each of his 'Sovreign' children – Edward VI, Mary and Elizabeth – carved in a delightfully naive manner by some itinerant sculptor. The result, known as 'The Court of the Sovreigns', is both striking and unusual.

Cadhay's fortunes declined somewhat in the next century, and in 1737 it was bought by William Peere Williams, who considered it not only in need of repair, but out of date. He carried out a programme of modernisation which included the refacing of the north front, the insertion of sliding sash windows on three sides of the courtyard, the plastering over of most of the Tudor hearths throughout the house and, most drastic of all, the insertion of another floor in the great hall. Such was the fate of many a Tudor house in the eighteenth century. Apart from the uncovering in the early part of this century of most of the open Tudor hearths, Cadhay today remains largely as Peere Williams left it.

The long gallery is charmingly simple for a period when ornate decoration and plasterwork were fashionable

A charming feature of Bingham's Melcombe is the manner in which the buildings ramble unsymmetrically round the inner courtyard

Bingham's Melcombe

'Everything about it is old world,' wrote Reginald Bosworth Smith in 1905 about Bingham's Melcombe, the remote Dorset house he had recently bought. 'The peace of centuries seems to be brooding over it. They have passed over it with their myriad changes and chances, with their ceaseless ebb and flow, with the racket and the turmoil of all their half-realised hopes and fears, leaving it unchanged – one would almost say unchangeable.'

The house lies in a lush green valley at the head of the Devil's Brook, between Coombe Hill and Henning Hill, to the south-west of Blandford. The first indication that one has arrived is a pair of gate piers just off the road, each surmounted by a stone eagle in the act of taking flight. The eagles are the crest of the Bingham family, who first came here in the thirteenth century, having inherited the land through marriage from the powerful Dorset family of Turbeville, immortalised by Hardy as the d'Urbevilles. The Binghams remained in residence till 1895, adding their name to that by which the property was formerly known – Melcombe, from 'mele', a mill, and 'combe', a valley.

The two-storey oriel which dominates the hall range is the most striking feature of the house

154

An archway of Purbeck stone divides the oriel from the main hall

Having passed through the gates, a short drive leads the visitor down to the gatehouse. Since some eighteenth-century Bingham gave this five sash windows surmounted by keystones, one might be excused for believing it to be a two-storey Georgian cottage. A closer look, however, at the gabled ends, the great buttresses and the massive central pointed archway, soon reveals both its probable age and its true nature, exciting one to move on and find out what lies within.

As it turns out, the gatehouse, which dates from the late fifteenth or early sixteenth century, forms one side of the manor house, which is of the courtyard type, with the east side left open. Its massive and simple form provides a stark contrast to the beauty of the buildings which ramble unsymetrically round the court. Roofs and gables are at different levels, no two windows seem to be the same, the gatehouse sits at a crazy angle, there does not appear to be a straight line anywhere and, to cap it all, the courtyard is on two levels, the hall range being raised up on a terrace and reached by two short flights of stone steps. Banks of hydrangeas and lavender abound and few of the stone surfaces are without a climber of some kind. The whole effect is enchanting.

The most striking feature of this inner court is the celebrated two-storey oriel which dominates the hall range, almost amounting to a small wing. Judging from the heraldic glass in its windows, this was probably built c.1554, when the early Tudor great hall was remodelled. It is a remarkable piece of architecture. To begin with there is a five-light mullioned window, the centre light of which is twice as broad as the others. Above this, at first-floor level, is an elaborately-carved coat of arms of the Bingham family, supported by fat cherubs, with scrolls and acanthus leaves all round. Finely decorated side shafts, which begin at the bottom of this panel, rise up to enclose a four-light window immediately above, before continuing on their way to emerge as pinnacles above the line of the gable. The whole wing, which is of silver-grey limestone with the decoration carved in honey-coloured Ham Hill stone, is flanked by slim pillars which soar upwards to rise above the roofline bearing on top of them the Bingham eagles once again ready for their flight. 'It is,' wrote Mr Bosworth Smith, 'a very dream in stone.'

East of the oriel is the entrance porch which leads straight into the hall. This retains little of its original character, having been largely remodelled, both in the sixteenth

The hall has been largely
remodelled. In the sixteenth
century it was divided
horizontally, while in the
eighteenth the east end, where
the screens would have stood,
was rebuilt to provide a library
and upstairs drawing room

The ancient yew hedge
in the garden

century, when it was divided horizontally, and in the
eighteenth century when the east end, where the screens
would have stood, was rebuilt to provide a library and
upstairs drawing room. The oriel, however, does at least
retain its original openings. Its full width is open to the
hall through a wide Gothic archway with a moulded four-
centred head springing from delicately carved capitals.
Rather than being just a recess, it is a small low-ceilinged
chamber in which the master of the house and his family
could eat apart from their retainers in the hall, a change
from medieval eating practices.

Apart from the drawing room, to the west of the hall,
the rest of the house is a hotch-potch of later periods. But,
in spite of this, the atmosphere of Bingham's Melcombe
remains essentially medieval.

Two views from the south-east. One of Pitchford's best features is the roof, tiled with beautiful sandstone slates

Pitchford Hall

The best place to get a good view of Pitchford Hall is from the road to the south which leads out of Acton Burnell towards Shrewsbury. Just outside the hamlet of Pitchford, a small lodge on the left marks the site of the original drive, now no more than a farm track leading into the fields beyond. From here one can look down across rolling farmland to a remarkable timber-framed mansion which lies at the bottom of the hill, its sparkling black and white exterior and sweeping sandstone-tiled roofs, topped by clusters of star-shaped brick chimneys, framed dramatically against a background of hardwoods. Looking at it for the first time, one cannot doubt that here must be, as Sir Nikolaus Pevsner calls it, 'the most splendid piece of black and white building in Shropshire.'

In the small church of St Michael, which stands next to the house, is an unusual monumental effigy of a knight, seven feet long and cross-legged, carved of oak. This rare survival marks the tomb of John de Pitchford, who died in 1285, and it serves as a reminder that in medieval times a family of that name held the manor. There is no record of

Some of the grotesque carvings which decorate the exterior woodwork

the house they lived in between 1284 and 1431, when the manor passed out of their hands, but the likelihood is that the present house was built on its site. It was probably begun soon after 1549 when John Sandford, a local carpenter, is recorded as having obtained the lease of a tenement in Pitchford 'during the building of a mansion place.' Its builder was Adam Ottley, a member of a family of rich Shrewsbury wool merchants who had bought the manor in 1473, and the structure he erected was of two storeys, designed on an E-shaped plan. The original entrance front, facing south, is now the garden side of the house.

The diagonal strut is the overwhelming motif of the exterior, the 'lozenge within lozenge'

This consists of two unusually long side wings which project forward some seventy feet on either side of a central porch and, being the same length as the width of the main block, enclose a square forecourt. Rather curiously, the west of these wings, which originally contained the offices, is set at a slightly oblique angle instead of joining the main block at right angles like its eastern counterpart. It is also structurally quite different, being much simpler in detail, and having no jetty at first-floor level. The most likely reason for this disparity is now thought to be that the west wing was actually built around part of the medieval manor house.

If the detail on the west wing is unremarkable, consisting of simple close-studded timbering, this is far from the case on the other two ranges. Here the timber framing consists of rectangular panels subdivided by diagonal struts, the whole forming an elaborate pattern of diamond shapes, 'lozenges within lozenges', Pevsner calls them. Other decoration includes a rather fanciful shaped gable above the central porch, with wavy supports carved with quatrefoils, and various carved figures and heads at the base of the gables on the east side.

The interior of Pitchford is unremarkable, having been heavily restored in the Elizabethan style of panelling and beams in the nineteenth century. There is, however, one other feature which, though of a later date than the main house, is of an eccentric enough nature to merit a passing mention. On the high ground to the south of the house stands a vast and ancient lime tree, whose great branches support an enchanting square timber-framed summer house. A view of the hall and grounds at Pitchford, dated 1714, shows this to have been in existence at that time, and the probability is that it was built either by Sir Francis Ottley or his father, Sir Thomas, in the early seventeenth century. The interior, which is delightfully decorated in the Gothic taste, with very pretty plasterwork, is a later insertion of the eighteenth century.

The early seventeenth-century
tree house

The Gothic interior of the tree
house, inserted in the
eighteenth century

The south front from across the garden, showing Sir George Trenchard's building of c.1600 with its great mullioned windows. The tower, garderobe turret and the length of wall linking them are from the early sixteenth century

The parlour with its carved wood chimney-piece in which central panels feature the figures of Hope and Justice, flanked by the three estates of feudal man: knight, squire and manservant

Wolfeton House

'In going out of Casterbridge by the low-lying road which eventually conducts to the town of Ivell, you see on the right hand an ivied manor house, flanked by battlemented towers, and more than usually distinguished by the size of its many mullioned windows. Though still of good capacity, the building is somewhat reduced from its original grand proportions; it has, moreover, been shorn of the fair estate which once appertained to its Lord, with the exception of a few acres of parkland immediately around the mansion. This was formerly the seat of the ancient and knightly family of the Drenghards, or Drenkhards, now extinct in the male line . . .' Thus did Thomas Hardy, in 'A Group of Noble Dames', describe Wolfeton House, ancient seat of the great Dorset family of Trenchard, a beautiful and romantic house which stands in wooded meadowland, close to the banks of the river Frome. The ivy has since been removed, the Thimblebys have replaced the Trenchards, but otherwise the exterior has changed little. Even so, as Hardy intimates, it is but a ghost of its former self.

The Trenchards, who built Wolfeton, were a family of Wessex landowners who made a fortune from extensive sheep farming. Sir John Trenchard inherited the property from his mother in 1480, and the fact that his son, Thomas, was able to entertain the Archduke Philip of Austria and Joanna of Castile there in 1506 would appear to suggest that a house of some size was already in existence. Apart from the gatehouse, however, nothing has survived from the fifteenth century. The latter is one of the house's most striking features, a massive rectangular building of silver-grey stone with fat round towers at the north-east and south-east corners, and with a gate passage through it from east to west. The towers, which are structurally independent with dovecots in their upper storeys, are the earliest part of the structure, dating from the time of Sir John Trenchard. High up on a chimney stack on the north wall is an inscribed panel which gives the date of the gatehouse itself as being 1534. It reads: 'HOC OPUS FINITUM EST ANNO DNI MDXXXIIII'. There are two doors within the arched entrance. That on the south side opens onto a

The nineteenth-century staircase
and part of the entrance hall

winding stair with steps of solid oak, that on the north into a dark chapel containing some interesting panels carved with the signs of the Zodiac.

'I came out of the gatehouse,' wrote Lord David Cecil, after a visit here a few years ago, 'to find myself confronted by another building, also antique-looking, but of a later date. A tall battlemented tower faced me looking eastwards: and behind it facing south a grey beautiful mullioned façade, part medieval, part Elizabethan . . . I was to learn that originally it formed part of a large grander structure.' This was described by John Hutchins in 1774 in his *History of Dorset*: 'The ancient seat of the Trenchards here is a noble building, and in the time when it was built perhaps the best in the country.' The house he described, which was built by Sir Thomas Trenchard and his great-grandson Sir George Trenchard, was arranged around a courtyard in which the gatehouse formed the east range, and a chapel the north range. Unfortunately the latter fell into ruins at the end of the eighteenth century and was demolished, and between 1822 and 1828 the west range and a large part of the south range were also pulled down. Enough architectural detail has survived, however, particularly on the beautiful south façade, to suggest that, when complete, Wolfeton must have been a building of great individuality and interest.

After the demolitions of the nineteenth century Wolfeton fell into a state of dereliction, and remained so until 1862 when it was bought by a Mr W. H. Weston. The interior which we see today is the result of the extensive programme of restoration and remodelling which he carried out. Sadly the hall, which extended east from where the present entrance hall is situated, is one of the rooms which has disappeared. 'The Hall is large,' wrote Hutchins, 'and, as all the principle rooms, is adorned with wainscot and fretwork. On the wainscot are carved over the chimney 14 Kings of England, which are said to resemble their figures in the first edition of Russell's History of England, ending with Charles I. Mr Aubrey, in

The sixteenth-century doorway
to the great chamber on the first
floor

The carved doorcase between
the parlour and the screens
passage

The fifteenth-century gatehouse, all that remains of the house Sir John Trenchard inherited in 1480

his Miscellanies, says that on November 3, 1640, the day the Long Parliament began to sit, the sceptre fell from the figure of Charles I while the family and a large company were at dinner in the Parlour.' The interior of the main building now consists of a vaulted entrance hall, parlour and dining room, with a great chamber above them. The former rooms are virtually all reconstructions and are notable for their abundance of carved woodwork from the sixteenth and seventeenth centuries, which was preserved from the old house and used to make door surrounds and chimney-pieces, cornices and panelling. The monumental stone staircase leading up to the great chamber is also a nineteenth-century restoration, though it closely follows the general form of the late sixteenth-century one. At the top is a very fine doorway from the landing into the great chamber which has a late sixteenth-century stone surround with Corinthian side pilasters. The frieze has an unusual carved enrichment of honeysuckle, acanthus and roses, a design which occurs at Longleat and which Mark Girouard has suggested may be the work of Allen Maynard, a Frenchman who was working for the Thynne family from 1563.

The great chamber itself, which occupies the whole of Sir George Trenchard's late sixteenth-century west extension, was, even in Hutchins' day, divided into several rooms. 'The upper apartment had a lofty coved or vaulted ceiling . . . which unfortunately has long been destroyed: but three of its large pendants still preserved are covered with tracery, and shew that it equalled and probably surpassed in richness of detail those of the lower rooms . . . and in one of the several bedrooms into which it is now divided is the original sculptured stone chimneypiece.' This room is now in the process of being restored, as far as possible to its original form, by the present and enormously enthusiastic owner, Captain Nigel Thimbleby.

Early Tudor windows to the
right of the garderobe turret

The south front still retains the original mullioned and transomed windows of the Tudor hall and of the gabled projection containing the great chamber

Herringston Manor

In no way could one's first view of Herringston prepare one for what lies within. Approaching it from the north, along a narrow road which heads out of the suburbs of Dorchester into rolling wooded countryside, one comes across the house quite suddenly, its drive meeting the road at a point where it takes a sharp turn to the left. The prospect is of a simple Gothic house of the nineteenth century, built of Portland ashlar, with a battlemented centre and gables which oddly overlap it. The latter are the only clue that all is not quite as it might at first seem.

In fact the origins of Herringston date back to the fourteenth century when Walterus Herung de Winterborne was granted a licence, in 1336, to crenellate his manor house. 'The ancient and Knightly family of Herring,' John Hutchins tells us in his *History of Dorset*, 'was of considerable note, and had large possessions in this county.' The likelihood is that, although there are today no visible features in the house attributable to that date, the main structure stems from Herring's original mansion. This was built round a courtyard with a gatehouse on the north side. In

1495 the property was acquired by a family called Williams who, over the next hundred years, as good as rebuilt Walter Herring's house. Of these, Sir John Williams, grandson of the purchaser, was of particular note. He succeeded to the estate in 1569 and 'by his building and other ornaments much beautified' the house. It was he who was responsible for the great chamber on the first floor, which he created partly out of the original hall and partly out of a new extension to the south of the main building.

The hall

The great chamber built by
Sir John Williams in the early
seventeenth century

Herringston remained as a courtyard house until the turn of the nineteenth century when Thomas Leverton, the architect of Bedford Square, London, was commissioned to design a new front. He pulled down the buildings round the north side of the quadrangle and filled in the space with the present entrance hall, dining room and library, thus converting the house into a solid block, which he fronted in the Gothic style. In 1899 further work was carried out when a new wing, now known as the Nursery Wing, was added on the east side. Today, so far as the exterior is concerned, the only part of Herringston where the Elizabethan flavour is preserved is the south elevation which still has the original mullioned and transomed windows both of the Tudor hall and of the gabled projection containing the great chamber.

A carved panel depicting a pair of scissors on a cupboard in the hall

Inside, Herringston has all the atmosphere of a house which has been inhabited by the same family for nearly five hundred years. It is comfortable and cluttered and has that delicious, indefinable smell that characterises so many ancient family seats, a mixture of old leather, polish and must. It contains two memorable rooms. The first is the hall which rises through two storeys on the south side of the house and serves as a wonderfully sunny and spacious sitting room. It is a delight. Family portraits cover the lofty walls. Weapons hang from the panelling. Squashy chairs abound, and a vast old Chesterfield slumps in front of the fireplace in which a woodburning stove is forever ablaze. There is not a surface which is not littered with books or family photographs. Once this room had a fine plaster barrel-vaulted ceiling, but this was sadly replaced with a flat one in the nineteenth century, and the only trace of it which remains is an outline in the west wall of the roof space.

The *pièce de résistance* at Herringston, however, is undoubtedly the first-floor great chamber built by Sir John Williams. It is a truly splendid room, some thirty-three feet long and seventeen feet wide, lit by a large three-sided window which juts out at its southern end, and, for

A panel on the wainscot, which is carved all over with figures drawn largely from the Bible and from myth

its carved wainscotting and elaborately carved barrel-vaulted ceiling, must lay claim to being one of the finest of its type in England. The plasterwork, which can be dated as being before 1610, is of the most exuberant kind, in many ways reminiscent of that in the Music Room at Stockton House, Wiltshire, the imagination of the plasterer having evidently once again run riot. The main ceiling, which springs from a moulded cornice with a frieze enriched with plain shields, consists of twenty-four square panels arranged in a rectangular pattern of ribs filled with images of flowers, leaves, animals, birds, fish and myth-ical creatures, among them a swan, a griffin, a boar, a pelican and three interlaced fish. There are further quaint reliefs of animals in the wall spaces above the frieze at each end of the room. At the north end can be seen a camel, a rhinoceros and an elephant; at the south end a lion and an antelope, and scenes of bear and bull baiting. In the centre of the ceiling, at intervals, are five pendants of which the central one has a particular charm. It consists of four curved bands enclosing an apple tree in full fruit, with a boy climbing up the trunk; between the bands are curved pedestals with three-quarter figures of boys eating

Panel from the wainscot depicting Adam and Eve

Further details of plasterwork at Herringston

apples, while four more boys, also eating apples, sit astride the pedestals with their feet dangling down. The carving of the wainscotting is equally rich, each panel depicting a mythical or biblical subject, including Hope, Sisera, Samson, Judith, Ruth, and Hercules.

Looking at the great chamber, which has survived in its entirety, and then reading Hutchins' account of the house, published in 1803, which describes the hall as being 'paved with Portland stone and ornamented with grotesque figures in the wainscot', only a few of which remain, leads one to wonder what other delights may have disappeared in the course of the nineteenth century.

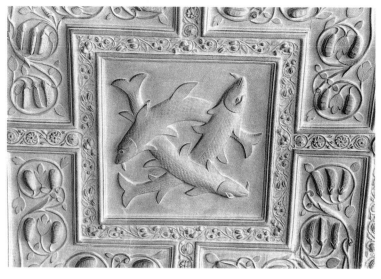

The ceiling of the great chamber
is covered with twenty-four
square panels carved with
images of flowers, leaves, birds,
fish and animals

180

The figures of
Hope and Charity
carved on the stone
chimney-piece

The elaborately carved
wainscotting at
Herringston

The south front is dominated by timber-framing. The polygonal stair turret and gabled bay bear the date 1615, while the adjoining wing on the left was added in the nineteenth century

Rainthorpe Hall

When the Hastings family moved into Rainthorpe Hall in the 1930s, they were returning to land which had been owned by their forefathers nearly a thousand years before. From them it had passed into the hands of a family called Appleyard, who built some kind of hall-house there in the fifteenth century. This was almost completely destroyed by fire soon after 1500. Some years later it was rebuilt and passed to the Chapman family. It was this house which in 1579 was bought by Thomas Baxter, a prosperous local barrister, who proceeded to completely remodel it.

It is an impressive building, E-shaped and built basically of brick with some timber framing at first-floor level. Particularly striking is the porch, set some way off centre, with big mullioned and transomed windows and polygonal angle-shafts. It is pierced by a perpendicular entrance arch which would appear to be of a date much earlier than the late sixteenth century, giving credence to the theory that Baxter merely enlarged and modernised an existing structure rather than built a new one. To the left of the porch is a two-storey gabled bay added in 1586. The south front of

Some of the fine panelling in the first-floor great chamber

the house is broken by a polygonal stair turret and a gabled bay which bears the date 1615. The wing which adjoins it to the left was added in the late nineteenth century.

The ground floor of the central block is taken up by the great hall, which rises only one storey. When built it would have been divided by the screens, with the kitchen, buttery and pantry to its right. Today it is one long room, the walls on either side of the screens passage and between the service rooms having been removed in the 1930s. Opposite the main entrance of the hall, the stair turret leads up to the great chamber, while beyond this, across a small landing, is the original solar, now a bedroom.

Everywhere in Rainthorpe are carved panels, pieces of stained glass and decorated chimney-pieces, which seem to have been inserted haphazardly. Most of these originate from a time when the house was owned by two famous collectors and antiquaries, first by the Hon. Frederick Walpole, a younger son of the third Earl of Orford, who lived there between 1853 and 1878, and then by Sir Charles Harvey who succeeded him. Almost every room contains some contribution from these two men, adding greatly to the charm and atmosphere of the house.

The single-storey great hall was once divided by screens, with the kitchen, buttery and pantry to its right. The walls on either side of the screens passage and between the service rooms were removed in the 1930s to make one long room

Overleaf: the east front. Rainthorpe is built on the E plan characteristic of Elizabethan houses of this date

Please
DO NOT PARK
IN THE
FORECOURT

Two views of the south-west front, the asymmetrical design of which gives it a striking appearance

Benthall Hall

The charming sixteenth-century manor house of Benthall stands upon a rise high above the river Severn, overlooking an area of England which has been called the birthplace of the Industrial Revolution. Little more than a mile to the east lies Coalbrookdale, where in 1709 Abraham Darby pioneered the smelting of iron with coke. Closer still stands the most famous industrial monument in Britain, the world's first iron bridge, with its massive span of one hundred feet, rising to forty feet above the river. At Brosely, on whose outskirts the house is to be found, John Wilkinson, father of the South Staffordshire iron trade, built the first iron barge in 1787. The Shropshire Coalfield begins at its very gates. For almost a hundred years Benthall looked out on a sky which was forever full of 'columns large of thick sulpherous smoke' which belched out from 'the red and countless fires' of a thousand furnaces. Such a vision is far removed from what a visitor to the house today will find, for though some industry has survived and a power station has sprung up to the north, the landscape surrounding the house is essentially pastoral.

189

Sheep graze in the meadows, and in the gardens wild flowers abound.

The early history of Benthall, the name of which is derived from Anglo-Saxon words meaning a field overgrown with bent grass, is sketchy. The family dates back to the twelfth century, but nothing is known of the previous house on the site which they occupied. Traditionally the present building is said to have been begun in 1535 by William Benthall, but the style of architecture points to a later date. What is likely is that either William's son, Richard, or his grandson, Lawrence, made extensive alterations in about 1580 which gave it its existing appearance. It is built of local sandstone and though the exterior is very plain, it is immediately striking. This is particularly true of the south-west front which has scarcely changed over the years. It is asymmetrical in composition, with a roofline of five gables, mullioned and transomed windows and clusters of tall moulded brick chimney stacks. Projecting outwards, two on the south front and one on the west, are three polygonal bay windows, each of two storeys in height and surmounted by a low parapet. Between the former two is the entrance porch. None of these are symmetrically placed, either in relation to the gables or to each other, yet the result is a most picturesque composition.

Despite damage by various fires, and alterations carried out in the eighteenth and nineteenth centuries, Benthall still contains many of its original features. A hiding-place in the entrance porch, for example, bears witness to the fact that the Benthalls were a family of recusants, ready to shelter any fugitive Catholic priest during times of persecution. Similarly, five stone tablets, thought to allude to the five wounds of Christ, in the form of a quincunx above the door in the west wall, served as a sign to strangers that the house was owned by Catholic sympathisers.

Within, there is some good original panelling in the library and in the Oak Dining Room, which also has a fine overmantel of c.1630, but the two best features are un-

The west drawing room, which dates from 1630, has had its panelling painted white. It is notable for its elaborately decorated plaster ceiling, overmantel and frieze

Carvings on the staircase

doubtedly the staircase and the west drawing room. The former was built in 1618 and is richly carved. The massive newel posts at the corners of the balustrade are in the form of grotesque heads while the balustrading takes the form of pierced strapwork panels. The panelled west drawing room, now painted white, dates from 1630 and is notable for its elaborately decorated plaster ceiling, overmantel and frieze. The latter is particularly ambitious with roundels depicting a variety of animals, such as a lion, a griffin, a horse and a stag, and between them birds holding one end of the drapery that forms part of the scrollwork.

The Benthalls occupied the house till the middle of the eighteenth century when it passed to a female cousin, and thence to her husband's family. Thereafter it had many different tenants until 1934, when it was once again bought by a Benthall. It was handed over to the National Trust in 1958, and the family are still in residence.

The staircase is dated 1618. It is richly carved, with newel posts in the form of grotesque heads and balustrading taking the form of pierced strapwork panels

The gatehouse was built from orange-yellow Guiting stone, from a local quarry, by Sir Richard Tracy

Stanway

'I can't remember anyone who didn't fall under the spell of Stanway,' wrote Lady Cynthia Asquith in her memoirs *Remember and Be Glad*. 'As a child I loved my home precisely as one loves a human being – loved it as I have loved very few human beings. I could never go away without a formal leave-taking. "How are you," I would ask on return, gazing up at the gabled front to absorb its beauty like a long, lovely draught, and I fancied that it smiled back a welcome.' It is only necessary to visit the house once to understand the fascination of this exquisite many-gabled Tudor-Jacobean mansion which nestles at the foot of a steep wooded hill.

The great sixty-light west oriel dates from about 1640

The manor of Stanway originally belonged to the Abbey of Tewkesbury, and had done so since the foundation of the Abbey in 715 by two brothers called Odo and Dodo. Early in the sixteenth century the estate was acquired by Richard Tracy, M.P. for Wootton Bassett. The antiquary John Leland, in his *Itinerary*, speaks of the Abbots of Tewkesbury being the owners of 'a fair manor-place' east of the church.

Richard Tracy was evidently content with the house as he found it, and it was left to his successor, Sir Paul Tracy, to enlarge and improve it. In about 1580 he built the west front and the hall. The hall is a particularly beautiful room owing to its abundance of windows. But it is the sixty-light west oriel which is undoubtedly the glory of the room, with, as Cynthia Asquith described, 'its hundreds of latticed panes, so mellowed by time that whenever the

One of a pair of classical pedimented doorways on the north side of the gatehouse

Detail of the west front

sun shines through their amber and green glass the effect is of a vast honeycomb and indeed at all times and in all weathers of stored sunshine.'

Stanway is built on an unusual L plan, the most likely explanation for which is that the west and south fronts were designed so as to incorporate pre-existing structures, namely Abbot Cheltenham's house and another lodging built by him to the east. One sees a long, elegant building of two storeys, faced with the same beautiful ashlar as the west front and topped by a charming parapet in a strap-work pattern of linked arches.

It was Sir Paul Tracy's son, Sir Richard Tracy, who was responsible for one of the most memorable features of Stanway, its extraordinary gatehouse. A mixture of the classical and Gothic, it consists of a three-storey elevation with three shaped Dutch gables on each side topped by the Tracy emblem of scallop shells. Approached from the south, it has a grandiose appearance, with a Tudor arch-way flanked by fluted columns and surmounted by a double pediment rising to the height of the centre gable and featuring the Tracy arms. Though the architect re-mains unknown, it has been suggested that it could poss-ibly be the work of Timothy Strong or his son Valentine, two local master masons.

Overleaf: a view of the west front of Stanway from the tower of the parish church

The hall is one of the lightest of its kind in the country owing to its abundance of windows. It has been considerably altered, but the ceiling is certainly of late medieval character

The gatehouse, seen through the courtyard arch

The magnificent two-storey hall with its gallery joining the two wings of the house

Hardwick Hall

High above the M1 motorway, Hardwick Hall dominates the Derbyshire countryside like a great galleon. On dark days it stands silhouetted against the sky, massive and mysterious. When the sun shines, its rays reflected in the complex arrangement of windows, the whole house glitters. Thus it has stood since 1598, the year of its completion, a monument to its builder, Elizabeth, Countess of Shrewsbury.

Best remembered as Bess of Hardwick, she was born at Hardwick in 1527, the daughter of John Hardwick, the owner of a small manor house and a few hundred acres. At the age of thirteen she went into the service of a grand Derbyshire family, that of Sir John and Lady Zouche of Codnor Castle. In 1543 she married a cousin, Robert Barlow, who died soon after, leaving her a small inheritance. As a childless widow, she continued to serve in great households, including that of the Marchioness of Dorset, the mother of Lady Jane Grey. Here she married, in August 1547, an extremely rich and elderly widower, Sir William Cavendish of Cavendish, Suffolk. In the ten years

Hardwick from the south, one of the four perfectly symmetrical fronts

202

'Like a great old castle of romance,' wrote Lord Torrington after a visit to Hardwick in 1789. 'Such lofty magnificence! And built with stone, upon a hill! One of the proudest piles I ever beheld!'

of their marriage she bore him six surviving children, and persuaded him to sell all his existing property and invest instead in land in the neighbourhood of Hardwick. Among his purchases were the house and estate of Chatsworth, which, along with a substantial proportion of his other property, she inherited on his death in 1557. By the time she embarked, two years later, upon her third marriage, she was a woman of considerable wealth.

Her wedding to William St Loe, a Gloucestershire landowner and favourite of the new Queen, Elizabeth I, was politic. He was Captain of the Royal Guard and Chief Butler of England, an important court appointment, and Bess soon found herself firmly ensconced in Royal circles. On Sir William's death, in the winter of 1564–65, she caught the eye of one of the most powerful men in the land. George Talbot, sixth Earl of Shrewsbury, was head of one of the oldest, grandest, and richest families in England. Master of eight important houses, he also owned coal mines and lead works, a shipyard, a glassworks, and had interests in iron and steel. Their marriage in 1567 was akin to the merging of two major corporations. It was to end with the Earl hating Bess and with their subsequent separation, a situation which was responsible for the building of Hardwick as we see it today.

The chimneypiece and doorway
by Thomas Accres in
the Green Velvet Room,
made of alabaster, blackstone
and other Derbyshire marbles
Far right: One of Hardwick's
superb doorways

The Queen of Scots Room:
Mary, Queen of Scots never came to
Hardwick but it is likely that
the panelling in this room was
brought here in the late
seventeenth century from
the apartment at Chatsworth
in which she was imprisoned

There were several reasons for the collapse of the marriage. The first was the Queen's decision to appoint Shrewsbury as custodian of Mary, Queen of Scots. Mary was a constant source of intrigue, so from that moment on Bess and her husband were living in a state of continuous tension. Secondly, Bess arranged a marriage between one of her daughters and the Earl of Lennox who, as the brother of Mary, Queen of Scots' murdered husband, Lord Darnley, had a possible claim to the throne. This infuriated Elizabeth and seriously embarrassed Shrewsbury, who was also angry at the amount of time and money Bess was spending on Chatsworth, which she was remodelling on a magnificent scale. All these matters combined to cause a complete breakdown of the marriage in 1584. Since Shrewsbury then chose to dispute his wife's ownership of Chatsworth, she moved to Hardwick, having bought the house and estate from her brother James in 1583.

Bess built two houses at Hardwick. The first is now known as Hardwick Old Hall, a ruin since the eighteenth

Part of the elaborate
painted plaster frieze in
the High Great Chamber

century. Work on it was begun in about 1585, and by 1590
the small manor house on the hill, in which she was born,
had been transformed into a large rambling mansion. Bess
was evidently dissatisfied with it, for when her husband
died in November of that year, an event which increased
her income by more than a third, she almost immediately
began work on a new and far more spectacular house, the
foundations of which were laid within a hundred yards of
the old, still uncompleted building.

Looking at Hardwick today, it is hard to believe that the
core of the house was completed in just two and a half
years. This was possible largely because almost all of the
building materials were available locally. Stone came from
a quarry halfway up the drive, slate from sites on the
Cavendish estates, lead from workings owned by Bess's

son William, iron from her own furnace, and glass from her substantial glassworks. The enormous trees needed for floors and roofs came from a variety of sources, the farthest afield being Chatsworth. Work was begun at the beginning of December 1590. In October 1597, Bess moved into an architectural masterpiece, since called 'the precursor of much modern architecture'. Here she remained until her death in 1608.

Many would argue that Hardwick is the finest house in England. It is certainly the supreme example of Elizabethan architecture, combining as it does three of its most notable characteristics and taking them to their extreme. It is perfectly symmetrical, the west front exactly matching the east, and the north the south. Then, as one moves around the exterior, the deceptively simple plan – a narrow rectangle surrounded by six towers – creates an elaborate illusion of shifting shapes and patterns. Finally, the importance and wealth of its owner is shouted to the world by the almost relentless use of the most expensive material available at the time – glass. There are huge windows in other great Elizabethan houses, but not on the same scale as those at Hardwick. The result is breathtaking, and inspired the now celebrated piece of doggerel – 'Hardwick Hall, more glass than wall.'

The inside of the house is equally exhilarating. The first surprise is to find the two-storey hall cutting straight through the centre of the house, rather than in its traditional disposition running parallel to the front. At its west end a screen of columns supports a gallery which provides communication between the two wings, while beyond this, on either side, are two staircases. These staircases are among the most memorable features of Hardwick for,

though their progress to the first floor is regular and unremarkable, thereafter they take off on a rambling itinerary through the centre of the house, winding backward and forward, through areas of shade and mystery, across spacious landings lit by huge windows, allowing here a magnificent view over the surrounding countryside, there a tantalising glimpse of some vast room or extraordinary piece of carving. Up and up they climb until they finally reach their conclusion in the north and south turrets some eighty feet from where they set out.

The staircases take one first to what were Bess's own suite of rooms. These, in later years the private apartments of her Cavendish descendants, the Dukes of Devonshire, include the original Low Great Chamber, a general room for sitting, eating and recreation. A typically Elizabethan inscription above the chimney-piece reads 'THE CONCLUSION OF ALL THINGS IS TO FEARE GOD AND KEEP HIS COMMAUNDEMENTES.'

One next ascends to the splendid state apartments, the most extraordinary of which is the High Great Chamber, a wondrous room filled with soft light and surrounded by an astonishing painted and modelled frieze. In Bess's day it was here that dinner and supper were served with great ceremony when she was keeping state. Adjoining it is the gallery, the largest of its kind surviving in England, and the only one to retain both its original tapestries and many of its original pictures.

Not even the dullest heart could fail to be touched by the romance and beauty of this great house, of which Sacheverell Sitwell once wrote, 'What wonders we have come from! All hidden, all enclosed behind the leaded windows, under the towers of Hardwick.'

The main staircase, made from local stone

The Shadrach Room, dominated by its extraordinary two-tier chimney-piece

Stockton from the south-west

Stockton House

In August 1826, William Cobbett rode from Salisbury to Warminster along the Wylye Valley. 'In coming from Salisbury,' he wrote in his diary of the 26th, 'I came up the road which comes pretty nearly parallel with the river Wylye, which river rises at Warminster and in the neighbourhood. The river runs down a valley twenty-two miles long . . . it is very fine in its whole length from Salisbury to this place [Heytesbury]. Here are watered meadows nearest to the river on both sides; then the gardens, the houses, and the cornfields. After the cornfields come the Downs . . .' This fertile green valley has changed little since Cobbett described it, and is still today a place of great beauty and seclusion in spite of its proximity to one of the main routes to the south-west, the busy A303. The village of Stockton, whose boundaries remain much the same as they were in the Domesday Book, lies a few miles to the south-east of Heytesbury. It has pretty thatched cottages, a fine Elizabethan farmhouse with a huge barn, a charming fourteenth-century church, and a manor house with some of the finest early Jacobean plasterwork in England.

Those who are lucky enough to get their first view of Stockton House late on a sunny summer afternoon are unlikely to forget it, for in the sunlight the lichen-covered Chilmark stone of which it is built takes on an almost eerie silver colour which seems to shimmer against the backdrop of two tall copper beeches. A closer investigation reveals a distinctive-looking house, rectangular in plan, with gables running regularly all round and the roof levels strictly even. What makes it particularly striking is the manner in which the walls are faced with alternating bands of stone and flint, which gives it a delightful stripey appearance. The west-facing entrance front is totally symmetrical, with two gables on either side of a three-storey porch. This rises to the level of the roof and is topped by a cresting of strapwork with a pierced ring as its centre. The east front has four gables and the north and south fronts both have three. The result is a pleasing exercise in regularity and symmetry, a trait which was by the turn of the seventeenth century becoming a more and more important feature of architecture.

The Music Room, which has one
of the finest plaster ceilings of its
kind in England. The porch in
the south-west corner is similar
to the one at Broughton Castle

'This respectable mansion,' wrote Colt Hoare in his
History of Wiltshire, 'was probably built by John Topp, as a
date in the building informs us, about the year 16...;' while
Burke, in his *Visitations*, writes 'We learn from the date
upon a stone that the house was built in 16—, but the two
last figures of the inscription having been erased, it is no
longer possible to fix the precise year of the century.' The
likelihood is that Stockton was built c.1600–1610 by John
Topp, whose 'family was raised to wealth and station by
success in trade as clothiers.' As one looks to the entrance
front today, the house remains very much as it was when
Topp built it, though there may originally have been an
open central court which was roofed over in the early
nineteenth century. A wing in chequerwork which extends to the north, and is known as the chapel wing, is
thought to be of a slightly later date, from the time of 'the
Great Rebellion when some of the ejected clergymen were
sheltered at Stockton by the Topps.' A similar wing was
added to the east side of the house by nineteenth-century
owners, who also built the water tower on the north side.

So far as the interior is concerned, even though the
original decoration of many of the rooms has been destroyed, the work that is left testifies to the sumptuousness
with which the house must once have been decorated
throughout. On the ground floor, that in the White Drawing Room provides a good clue as to the greater glories to
come. The ornamentation includes a stucco frieze with
strapwork and heads, and the initials I.M.T. for John Topp
and his wife Mary, while in the ceiling there are reminders
of the family's origins as clothiers. Spindles are placed
between the ribs as they spring from the cornice, while on
either side of the blank shields in the upper frieze are

teazles, which were used to draw out the wool. The
chimney-piece is particularly impressive, with a remarkable scrolled top flanking the coat of arms and seated
greyhounds on each side. The Elizabethan Room on the
same floor has a fine two-tier chimney-piece and a ceiling
in the design of which are included the Tudor coat of arms
and the initials ER in reverse on either side.

But the best plasterwork is to be found upstairs. For its
size there can be few rooms in England so elaborately
decorated as the Shadrach Room, so called because it is
dominated by a towering two-tier chimney-piece carved
with a relief of Shadrach, Meshag and Abednego, the
three Israelites Nebuchadnezzar had thrown into a fiery
furnace and who refused to burn. They are flanked by two
huge figures of soldiers. A beautifully detailed frieze of
pairs of winged horses runs round the room, and the
ribbed ceiling is carved with panels of varying shapes,
some square, some semi-circular, some heart-shaped,
filled with emblems of the Tudor rose, the thistle and the
fleur de lys.

The masterpiece of Stockton is unquestionably the
Music Room, formerly the great chamber, which for the
sheer brilliance of its plasterwork has few rivals in England. It is a spacious room, with large windows facing
south and west, panelled throughout with alternate rows
of large and small panels, broken up at intervals by fluted
pilasters. These support a frieze of acanthus which runs
beneath a cornice which, somewhat curiously, does not
touch the ceiling, the plasterwork continuing behind it,
suggesting perhaps that the woodwork was completed at
a slightly later date. Whoever the plasterer was, he let his
imagination run riot, creating across the ceiling a network

The porch in the Music Room

of interlacing diamonds and lozenges abounding in long-stalked flowers, varying from panel to panel. There are animals everywhere, boldly carved mythical beasts, swans, wild boar, hounds, deer and an elephant with a huge butterfly perched on its back. In the oriel in the north-west corner there are fish in the panels, and at its centre a large pendant with faces carved on each side. An impressive two-tier chimney-piece dominates the east wall, with a relief in the overmantel depicting the story of Adam and Eve. In the south-west corner is a richly carved porch of the type seen at Broughton Castle, with figures of Diana, Cupid and Athena standing on the top.

The pendant in the oriel recess and, below, details of plaster panels on the Music Room ceiling

The east elevation across the topiary garden

The south entrance front. The projection and recession of the bays, and the way in which the windows are set at different levels, give an impression of height

Chastleton

Few houses in England are as romantic as Chastleton, which has survived virtually unaltered since the death of its builder in 1632. Situated on a remote wooded ridge of the Cotswolds, it stands 600 feet above sea level, and from its topmost windows there are wonderful views over the surrounding countryside. Approaching from the direction of Moreton-in-Marsh, one catches a glimpse of stone parapets and gables peeping over the encircling trees. One's attention is next arrested by a charming stone dovecot, raised above segmental arches and topped by a cupola, sitting in a field to the right, and then, on the opposite side of the road, by a striking stone archway surmounted by a pediment. Beyond this, at the end of an overgrown drive, can be seen a gabled manor house of yellow-grey stone.

Chastleton dates back to the turn of the seventeenth century when, in 1602, Walter Jones, a rich and ambitious wool merchant who claimed a pedigree going back to Brutus, first King of Britain, and thence to Priam, King of Troy, bought the estate of Robert Catesby for £4,000. Catesby, a recusant who was later executed for his in-

volvement in the planning of the Gunpowder Plot, was forced to sell as a result of punitive fines he had suffered for his participation in the Earl of Essex's rebellion in 1601. Nothing is known of the house which he sold with the land, except that it was evidently not grand enough for the upwardly-mobile Jones. He decided to rebuild without delay. Whether he did so on the site of the old house or upon a new one is uncertain, but what he built is exactly what we see today.

It consists of a quadrangular house set round an inner court. On the south, entrance front, five narrow gables recede from the centre to massive staircase towers on either side. The eye is drawn up to a picturesque skyline broken by gables, tall chimneys and battlemented towers. The symmetry of the front is maintained by the expedient of having the principal entrance doorway hidden away in the side of the left-hand bay, much as it is at Burton Agnes, often regarded as Chastleton's sister house.

Though hidden from view the entrance doorway is an elaborate affair with fluted Doric pilasters and strapwork

The hall. The portrait above
the fireplace is of Walter Jones,
who built Chastleton in 1604

cresting. It leads into a small porch and thence to the
screens passage. To the left of this is a small panelled
parlour, in present use as a dining room, with the kitchen
and other offices beyond. Two arched openings lead into
the hall, a single-storey room dominated by a generous
bay window which fills it with a beautiful soft light. It is
decorated with simple panelling halfway up, above which
are whitewashed walls hung with family portraits, arms,
and a set of huge reindeer antlers attached to a wooden
head and painted body. Alongside the south wall is the
original eighteen-foot long refectory table, which was
made inside the hall itself. Apart from the screen, which is
elaborately carved with columns, satyrs, strapwork cresting and acanthus scrolls, the hall is a very plain room and
quite small in size, being only thirty-four feet by twenty-
one, an indication of the shrinking importance at this date
of the room which had been the dominant feature of a
house little more than half a century before.

The great chamber,
the most richly decorated room
in the house

The most important rooms at Chastleton are on the
upper floors. These are reached either by means of modern stairs in the east tower, or by the impressive Jacobean
oak staircase in the west tower which rises in short flights
with numerous landings, and upon which square balusters form a cage to the stairwell. On the first floor is the
magnificent great chamber, every inch of whose walls and
ceilings are covered with vigorous decoration. Not only
are the walls entirely panelled, but they are lavishly covered
with strapwork and arches in the Flemish style, and incorporate twenty-four paintings of Sybils and Prophets.
Pendants drip from the ceiling, emerging from a compli-
cated pattern of ribs filled with trailing vine leaves, fruit

and flowers. An impressive stone chimney-piece dominates the north wall, rising from floor to ceiling with the
arms of Walter Jones and his wife grandly carved in the
overmantel. Particularly beautiful is the State Room, a
small bedroom designed around a set of sixteenth-century
Flemish tapestries. Another bedroom which contains a
secret chamber is a reminder of the miraculous escape
during the Civil War of Walter Jones's grandson, Arthur,
an ardent Royalist, who was concealed there after the
disastrous Battle of Worcester in September 1651. As he
lay in hiding, his wife calmly entertained the Cromwellian
troops who were in pursuit and engineered his escape by
drugging their drinks with opium.

The Jacobean oak staircase in
the west tower

The top of the staircase in
the west tower

The State Room was designed
around the sixteenth-century
Flemish tapestries on the wall.
The blue and white needlework
bedcover and the hangings for
the four-poster bed were all
made at Chastleton

Finally, at the very top of the house, is the barrel-vaulted long gallery, which runs the entire length of the north front. The original wide pale oak floorboards still creak beneath one's feet, some of the panelling, divided into sections by fluted pilasters, survives, and the plaster-work of the ceiling, a network of interlacing ribs filled with daisies, roses and fleurs de lys, is of an unusual delicacy for so large a room.

The present owner of Chastleton, Mrs Clutton Brock, is a descendant through marriage of the Jones family, and it is her wish that after her death the house should go to the National Trust.

The long gallery, which runs
the entire length of the north front

The gatehouse, the last part of
the house to be completed

Burton Agnes

'Agnes Burton looks finely in the approach,' wrote Celia
Fiennes, and 'stands on a pretty ascent, we enter under a
Gate House built with four large towers into a Court,
which is large, in the middle is a Bowling green palisado'd
round, and the Coaches runns round it to the Entrance,
which is by ten steppes up to a Tarress, and there a pav'd
walke to the house, cut box and filleroy and laurell about
the Court . . .'

The name Burton Agnes, which Celia Fiennes so charmingly reversed, derives from the old English for 'fortified
manor' and the name of one of the five daughters of Roger
de Stuteville, builder of Burton Agnes Old Hall, which
dates from 1173 and still stands alongside its successor.
Since de Stuteville held the manor, Burton Agnes has
never once changed hands by sale, though it has passed
on several occasions from family to family through marriage. It was under such circumstances that it was inherited in 1355 by the Griffiths, a Welsh family who had

emigrated to Staffordshire in the thirteenth century, and a descendant of whom was the builder of the present house. Though Sir Henry Griffiths spent most of his early life involved with his estates in the midlands, in 1599 he was elected to the Council of the North, a position which required regular attendance at York. He decided in 1601 to build himself a stately new home at his Yorkshire manor.

We are left in little doubt as to the years during which the house was built, for the craftsmen who worked upon it left the dates of their labours well marked. The first of these, 1601, is carved in a panel just above the entrance

The entrance front. Like Chastleton, Burton Agnes is planned round a small internal court. The architect was Robert Smythson

227

doorway, along with the initials of Sir Henry and his wife. A little higher up the date 1602 appears, and is repeated, along with the year 1603, on the rainwater heads on the inner sides of the wings. In the south-east bedroom 1610 is carved in the frieze above the chimney-piece, a date which also appears on the gatehouse, which was the last part of the house to be completed. With its octagonal turrets capped by lead cupolas and bearing the arms of James I flanked by caryatids, the latter is purely ornamental, designed to set off the house and built of the same brick.

One approaches the house up a gentle slope flanked by an avenue of topiary bushes. Though both the bowling green noted by Celia Fiennes and the ten steps leading up to a terrace are now gone, the main façade is otherwise more or less as she would have seen it. With its mass of windows it is a splendid and confident structure. The compass-windows, which dominate the entrance front, are of particular interest in that they are bow rather than bay windows, and bow windows scarcely existed before the 1630s.

The great hall

Detail of the relief above the
chimney-piece in the drawing
room, depicting the Dance of
Death with the Saved and the
Damned

Within, as one would expect, a screens passage leads straight into the hall, where the plain eighteenth-century ceiling provides a stark contrast to the extravagance of the screen and chimney-piece, which Sir Nikolaus Pevsner described as 'the most crazily overcrowded screen and the most crazily overcrowded chimney-piece of all England.' So far as the former is concerned it is not so much the wooden screen itself that gives this impression, though it is elaborately carved and has a delightful frieze depicting the twelve tribes of Israel, but the massive bank of plaster-work above it. Within this allegorical figures, angels, knights in armour, costumed ladies, the twelve Apostles and the four Evangelists, all vie for position, reaching upwards to the very ceiling, against which the topmost figures appear to knock their heads. As for the chimney-piece, its decoration is equally fantastic, with a frieze illustrating the five senses and an elaborate relief telling the story of the Wise and Foolish Virgins.

At the east end of the hall an arched doorway opens into an antechamber, from which is reached the drawing room, notable for the relief above the chimney-piece which depicts the Dance of Death with the Saved and the Damned. This is dominated by the ghastly figure of a skeleton brandishing a spear. On the first floor the most interesting room is the Queen's State Bedroom, which has richly decorated panelling and a lovely plaster ceiling covered by an intricate design of intertwining fronds of honeysuckle. Above the chimney-piece is yet another allegorical panel portraying Patience, Truth, Constance and Victory. It is this room which is reputed to have been the centre of hauntings by Anne Griffiths, the youngest daughter of Sir Henry, who died after being attacked by robbers at the neighbouring village of Harpham. She asked on her deathbed that her head might always remain in the house which she so loved. When the family failed to carry out her wishes, they were disturbed by terrible wailings. These ceased as soon as the skull was interred within the walls of the house, and all subsequent attempts to

The staircase, similar to the one at Cranborne Manor, is of the continuous newel type, with the main posts being carried up in pairs interconnected by arches

The Queen's State Bedroom

remove it have resulted in similar occurrences. It is thought to be buried somewhere high up in the hall.

The second floor is dominated by the long gallery. Similar to the one at Chastleton, it has a richly decorated barrel-vaulted ceiling and runs the entire length of the main front. In the early nineteenth century much of the ceiling collapsed, and it was subsequently divided up into smaller rooms. It has recently, however, been completely restored.

Heraldic carving above
the entrance door showing
the date of building, 1602

The south, entrance front seen
from the top of the drive

The north front

Cranborne Manor

For sheer unspoiled loveliness, there are few houses in England to rival Cranborne Manor. Its history goes back to the turn of the thirteenth century. King John, a fanatical huntsman, was the owner of a prodigious number of hunting lodges, of which Cranborne was a favourite. The house which then existed probably dated back to the time of William Rufus, and was modest in size, for John decided to rebuild it, and c.1207–8 Ralph Neville, his chief forester, is recorded as having spent £67.6.4d on 'building the King's houses of Cranborne.'

When John Norden saw the hunting lodge at Cranborne between 1600 and 1610, it had fallen into ruins. Between 1608 and 1612 the then lord of the manor, Robert Cecil, first Earl of Salisbury, spent £3,048 on rebuilding King John's old hunting lodge.

The man who supervised the work was a master stone-mason called William Arnold, and he and Cecil ingeniously retained the remains of the old house, yet gave it the appearance of a completely new and symmetrical building. They raised the existing south-west stair turret

to above the line of the battlements and added an identical new turret to balance it at the south-west corner. Two smaller wings of lodgings were built. Grand mullioned and transomed windows replaced the small arched ones of the original. But most delightful of all are the classical three-bay arcaded loggias which they added to the north and south fronts. That on the north front is particularly enchanting, with its gaping lion-head gargoyles in the spandrels of the arches, its strapwork ornamentation, its shell niches surmounted by carved relief heads in extravagant frames, while on either side and above it the formerly plain stepped buttresses have been decorated with strapwork pilasters capped by obelisks. The final flourish to the north front is set by the two groups of tall diagonally-set brick chimneys, three in each, which rise starkly up above the roofline, their deep red colour contrasting beautifully with the silver-grey of the stone walls.

The great hall is the most noteworthy room in the house. Tall and spacious, it has fine oak panelling, a broad four-centred stone fireplace, and a gallery over the screens

The great hall

passage which has an oak front with arcaded panelling. In the south-west corner, a four-centred arch leads to the other great feature of the house, the early seventeenth-century oak staircase.

Robert Cecil barely lived to see the completion of the new Cranborne Manor, for he died in May 1612. His son William, the second Earl, however, entertained the King there often and lavishly.

When the Civil War broke out, William took the side of Parliament, a decision which had drastic results for Cranborne. Scarcely had he organised the shipping out of all the furnishings for safety than, on 23 May, 1643, the Marquis of Hertford and Prince Maurice arrived with the Royalist army. A memorandum of that date tells the rest of the story: 'When he [Mr Boothe, Lord Hertford's Steward] was told by SS [Sam Stillingfleet, Lord Salisbury's Steward] that the household stuff was removed, he swore he was a round-headed —— and that the army should be quartered there. When the Lord Marquis Hertford commanded that no hurt should be done Cranborne House, within half an hour after, 5 or 600 of the Prince's regiment broke into it in an instant, pulled out iron bars and casements, and carried away everything which was portable . . . They killed a hundred sheep, most of them in the house, leaving it more nasty than any slaughter house . . . Sir Ja. Hamilton on Wednesday returned with his regiment of horse and foot and defaced more of the house.' The worst of the damage was to the west wing, the cost of repairs to which would have been so high that the Earl decided to rebuild it from scratch. The work was begun in 1647, and the result was a two-storey block containing one room over a low ground storey, crowned by a massive and steep hipped roof.

Cranborne's heyday appeared to be over, and it began to fall into disrepair. For two hundred years it was as good as abandoned by the family. It was the second Marquis of Salisbury who, in 1863, decided to bring the old house back to life. Since that date the family have taken an increasing interest in Cranborne, and, thanks to skilful restoration and inspired gardening, it can never have looked more beautiful.

Grotesque masks on the north elevation

237

The staircase, similar to the one
at Burton Agnes, is a striking
and complex-looking structure,
with continuous square newel
posts converted above handrail
level into columns

GLOSSARY

BARGEBOARD: A projecting decorated board placed against the incline of a gable of a building and hiding the horizontal roof-timbers.

BAY: A division of a building, inside or outside, marked not by walls but units of vaulting, arches, roof compartments or windows.

BRACE: An inclined timber, straight or curved, introduced usually at an angle, to strengthen others.

BRACKET: A projection designed as a support.

BRESSUMER: A horizontal beam supporting a superstructure.

BUTTRESS: Masonry or brickwork built against a wall to provide stability or to counteract the outward thrust of an arch or vault.

CHEVRON: A zigzag form of ornamentation.

COLLAR-BEAM: Tie-beam applied higher up the slope of a roof.

CORBEL: A block of stone, or a piece of brickwork projecting from a wall to support a floor, roof, parapet, vault, or other feature.

CUSP: Projecting point between the foils in a foiled Gothic arch.

DIAPER: An all-over pattern usually of lozenge, square or diamond shapes.

FINIAL: The topmost feature, generally ornamental, of a gable, roof, pinnacle, or canopy.

FOIL: (TRE, QUATRE, etc.) A three, four or more-lobed ornamental infilling for a circle or arch-head.

GABLE: Triangular portion of wall at the end of a ridge roof: a Dutch gable is curved and shaped and surmounted by a pediment; a stepped gable has stepped sides.

GARDEROBE: Lavatory or privy in a medieval building.

HAMMERBEAM: Beams projecting at right-angles from a wall, to provide support for the vertical members and/or arched braces of a wooden roof.

KINGPOST: A vertical beam standing centrally on a tie-beam or collar-beam and rising to the apex of the roof to support the ridge.

LINENFOLD: Panelling carved to look like vertically folded linen.

LOGGIA: A covered arcade or colonnade open on at least one side.

MACHICOLATION: A projecting parapet on a castle wall or tower, with openings in the floor through which to drop missiles.

MULLION: A vertical post or other upright dividing a window into lights.

NEWEL: The central column from which steps of a winding staircase radiate, and also the principal posts at the angles of a square staircase which support the handrail.

ORIEL: A window projecting from an upper storey.

PARAPET: A low wall on bridge, castle, church, gallery or balcony, above the cornice.

PURLIN: A longitudinal horizontal beam or pole supporting the common rafters of a roof.

QUADRIPARTITE VAULT: A rib vault in which two diagonal ribs divide each bay into four compartments.

SOLAR: A parlour or private room in medieval and Tudor manor houses, usually at first floor level.

SPANDREL: The approximately triangular space between the outer curve of an arch and the rectangle formed by the mouldings enclosing it.

SQUINT: A hole cut in a wall to allow a view of the hall of a medieval house from places whence it could otherwise not be seen; often hidden by a mask.

STRAPWORK: Sixteenth and seventeenth-century flat interlaced decoration, seemingly derived from bands of cut leather.

TIE-BEAM: Beam connecting the two slopes of a roof.

TRACERY: Intersecting ornamental ribwork in the upper parts of Gothic windows, walls, screens and vaults.

TRANSOM: A horizontal bar of stone or wood across the openings of a window.

TRUSS: A group of strong timbers arranged as a supporting frame within the triangle formed by the sloping sides of a timber-framed roof.

UNDERCROFT: A vaulted underground room or crypt.

VAULT: Arched roof of stone.

WAGGON ROOF: A curved wooden rafter roof giving the appearance of the inside of a canvas tilt over a waggon.

WIND-BRACE: A diagonal timber brace, usually curved, crossing the rafters to strengthen the roof longitudinally.